"OVER A WIDE, HOT, . . . CRIMSON PLAIN"

THE STRUGGLE

FOR

THE BLISS FARM

AT

GETTYSBURG

July 2nd and 3rd, 1863

"OVER A WIDE, HOT, . . . CRIMSON PLAIN"

THE STRUGGLE

FOR

THE BLISS FARM

AT

GETTYSBURG

July 2nd and 3rd, 1863

by

Elwood W. Christ

Baltimore
Butternut and Blue
1994

Second Edition

ISBN 0-935523-31-6

Butternut and Blue

3411 Northwind Road
Baltimore, Maryland 21234
(410)-256-9220

DEDICATION

To my late parents Warren George Christ and Sarah Melinda (Strauss) Christ, the sixth generation of German immigrants who came to the Colony of Pennsylvania in 1733 and 1732, respectively.

When I try to write it I get stuck; in fact a battle is a plaguey poor thing to put on paper – somehow it won't <u>fight</u>!

Lieutenant Fiske
14th Connecticut Volunteers

Quoted in Henry S. Stevens, *Souvenir of the Excursions by the Society of the 14th Connecticut Regiment and Reunion at Antietam September, 1891.*

TABLE OF CONTENTS

ACKNOWLEDGMENTS

In the compilation of this study there were numerous individuals and institutions who rendered me invaluable assistance in the compilations of information. Unfortunately and unforgivably, due to great eagerness and enthusiasm on my part some have been overlooked by name, and to these folks I extend my sincere apologies.

First of all, acknowledgment goes to those people who had become entangled in the battles at Gettysburg, especially to those individuals, veterans and private citizens alike, whose sense of history initially preserved for posterity the battle ground and the personal experiences of those directly involved in the engagement.

Secondly, sincere thanks go to the following persons whose invaluable assistance and encouragement are truly appreciated: Dr. Walter L. Powell, Executive Director, Gettysburg Battlefield Preservation Association; Jerry D. Fairchilde, Archaeologist; Kathy Georg-Harrison, Historian, and Becky Lyons, Todd Bolton, and Scott Hartwig, Park Ranger-Interpreters, present or former employees at Gettysburg National Military Park/Eisenhower National Historic Site; Ed Guy, Roy Frampton, Clyde James, and Wayne Motts, Licensed Battlefield Guides; Edmund J. Raus, Jr., Historian, Manassas National Battlefield; Ted Alexander, Park Ranger-Historian, Paul Chiles, Interpretative Specialist, and Betty J. Otto, retired Curator, Antietam National Battlefield; William A. Frassantio; Drs. Charles Glatfelter and Bruce Bugbee, professors of History, Gettysburg College; Louise Arnold-Friend, Research Historian, Randy Hackenberg and Michael Winey, Photographic Archivists, and Dr. Richard Sommers, Archivist-Historian, at the U. S. Army Military History Institute, Carlisle Barracks, Pennsylvania; and Jeffrey W. Geiss, Surveyor with George K. Jones Associates, Towanda, Pennsylvania (who took time from his busy schedule to show me a copy of an old patent map which located the William Bliss farmstead in Bradford County).

The folks at the following institutions were very helpful in supplying obscure but crucial information: Fenton Historical Society, Jamestown, New York (especially the gentleman who remained after regular closing hours and directed me to the proper card files which provided the first real biographical leads to the William Bliss family and located the family grave site in Chautauqua County); Deed Offices and Mapping Departments at the Chautauqua County Court House, Mayville, New York and at the Bradford County Court House, Towanda, Pennsylvania; Old Colony Historical Society, Taunton, Massachusetts (especially the lady who had spread maps on the floor assisting me in locating the home of William's birth); the Probate and Deed Registry, Taunton; Town Hall, Rehoboth, Massachusetts; the Rehoboth Public Library; the curator of the Carpenter Family Museum, Rehoboth; and those folks who were kind enough to give me directions when I had become lost in the wilds of Pennsylvania, New York and Massachusetts.

Lastly I extend my thanks to Mr. Roger D. Hunt, Rockville, Maryland who graciously has given permission for the use of several photographs of participants as illustrations for this undertaking, and to the following organizations who have granted permission to quote passages from their collections/publications:

Macmillan Publishing Company [Lee's Lieutenants & R.E. Lee by Douglas S. Freeman; The Gettysburg Campaign by Edwin Coddington]

Morningside Bookshop Press [The Gettysburg Papers edited by Ken Bandy & Florence Freeland; Lieutenant General Richard Heron Anderson by Joseph Elliot; Grandfather's Journal by Austin Dobbins]

New Hampshire Historical Society [John B. Bachelder Papers]

University of Georgia Press [Berry Benson's Civil War Book edited by Susan W. Benson]

University of Texas-Austin, The Center for American History [Diary of James J. Kirkpatrick]

Stackpole Books [The Valiant Hours by Thomas Galway]

The Valley Forge Historical Society [Diary of George D. Bowen]

Houghton-Mifflin Company [Pickett's Charge by George Stewart]

Louisiana State University Press [Here Come the Rebels! by Wilbur Nye]

Nevertheless, their encouragement and assistance of the above does not relieve me of the responsibility of the accuracy and integrity of this study.

LIST OF ILLUSTRATIONS

Army of Northern Virginia (Confederate)

Army of the Potomac (Union)

The Field

LIST OF MAPS*

* Maps found within this work, drawn by the author, were based on a tracing of a Blue Print copy of the John B. Bachelder Maps of the field (scale: 1" = 200 ft) with modifications derived by comparing it to the Warren Commission, Bachelder, and modern 7.5 Minute U. S. Geological Survey maps of the area. Troop locations and movements were drawn, interpreted from the Official Records reports, unit histories, and from monument placements on the field. Troop movements as shown in Map 7 were partially derived from George R. Stewart's map, "The Advance (3:10–3:30 P.M.)," found in *Pickett's Charge: A Microhistory of the Final Attack at Gettysburg, July 3, 1863.*

INTRODUCTION

In his widely praised work, *Pickett's Charge: A Micro-history of the Final Attack at Gettysburg, July 3rd, 1863*, historian George R. Stewart wrote that "Enough deeds of valor were done around [the Bliss barn], that morning, to supply material for a small epic." Unfortunately, since the publication of his book in 1959, the struggle for the William Bliss Farm has not been researched or analyzed in depth, though what happened there rightly deserves a "small epic." The fight for the Bliss Farm played an important role in the battle, possibly just as important as that of the 20th Maine in the defense of Little Round Top.

Over a thirty-two hour period, troops fought for possession of the Bliss house and barn which were located in the middle of the no-mans land between Seminary and Cemetery ridges. However, the events and the soldiers who fought over them – primary topic of this book – have been all but forgotten, made anticlimactic by Pickett's Charge which traversed the farmstead in the afternoon of 3 July. Nonetheless, ramifications of the Bliss Farm skirmishes not only had a direct affect on the Confederate en echelon attacks on 2 July, they helped mold the outcome of Pickett's Charge.

In a final analysis, the failure of the Confederate attacks on the Union center on 2 and 3 July were not due simply to a lack of Confederate stamina and the tenacious defense of Union troops as many battle histories suggest. There were extenuating circumstances which included the fight over the Bliss Farm.

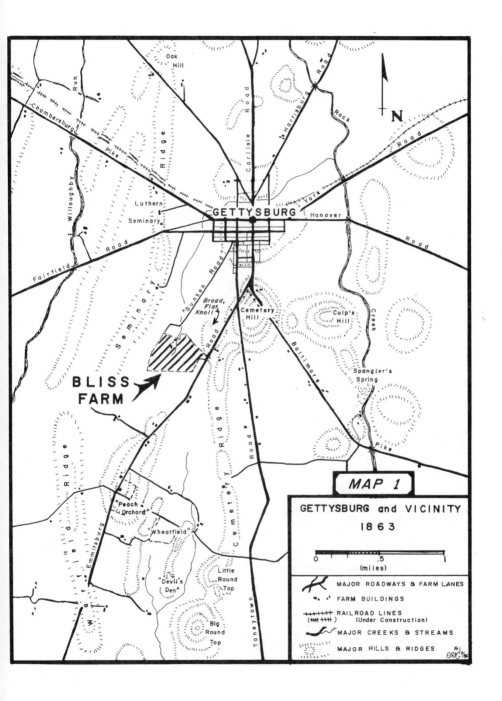

BLISS
FARM

GETTYSBURG

Luther
Seminary

Oak
Hill

Broad,
Flat
Knoll

Cemetery
Hill

Culp's
Hill

Spangler's
Spring

"Peach
Orchard"

"Wheatfield"

"Devil's
Den"

Little
Round
Top

Big
Round
Top

Chambersburg Pike

Willoughby Run

Fairfield Road

Seminary Ridge

Carlisle Road

Harrisburg Road

Rock Creek

York Road

Hanover Road

Baltimore Road

"Sunken Road"

Cemetery Ridge

Taneytown Road

Emmitsburg Road

Pike

N

```
 ┌─────────────────────────┐
 │        MAP 1            │
 └─────────────────────────┘

   GETTYSBURG and VICINITY
           1863

   0            .5           1
        (miles)
```

MAJOR ROADWAYS & FARM LANES

FARM BUILDINGS

RAILROAD LINES
(Under Construction)

MAJOR CREEKS & STREAMS

MAJOR HILLS & RIDGES

Chapter One

"... A CITADEL IN ITSELF."

The summer of 1863 was promising to be a long, dry one in south-central Pennsylvania. A farmer in Upper Adams County recorded in his diary during the latter part of May that the "ground was very dry [due to the lack of rainfall] for the past three weeks." Though the dry spell ended in June, many days that month were cloudy with temperatures unseasonably cool.[1] Undoubtedly, many a local farmers' outlooks for the upcoming growing season improved.

However, people in the greater Gettysburg area noticed some obscure articles which first appeared in the 15 June issue of the *Compiler*. A short piece on page two reported on the "Great Cavalry Clash of the War" that had taken place at a small rail stop known as Brandy Station, Virginia on 9 June. On page three, news had been received from Chambersburg, thirty miles to the west-northwest, that:

> there was some apprehension of a rebel raid there. Government stores were being placed on [rail] cars ready to be conveyed away at a moment's notice. It had been reported that Milroy's [Federal] detachment at Winchester [Virginia] had been attacked.

By the morning of the 26th, the residents of Gettysburg and the surrounding countryside came to the realization that the war was marching directly towards their doorsteps. Around the noon hour, townsfolk were alarmed by reports that the Confederates were only two miles from town out the Chambersburg Pike. "No one believed this," wrote Sarah M. Broadhead, "for they had so often been reported as just coming." However, any doubts were quickly swept away as the baggage wagons of Pennsylvania militia that had been sent to protect the local citizenry, came "thundering through the streets" of Gettysburg retreating to the east.[2]

In the early afternoon of that rainy Friday, elements of General Robert E. Lee's Army of Northern Virginia under the command of Major General Jubal A. Early routed a small force of green, untrained militia west of Gettysburg, and about mid-afternoon, Confederate cavalry followed by infantry galloped into town. A short time later the captured Yankee militiamen, who were corralled in front of the court house, allegedly were admonished by "Old Jubal," who said in so many words, "You boys ought to be home with your mothers and not out in the fields where it is dangerous and you might get hurt."[3] After realizing that their request for supplies could not be filled by the townspeople and after the burning of a railroad bridge and some railroad cars east of town, Early's troops continued on their way the following morning heading east towards the town of York and the Susquehanna River.

However, after only four days of relative quiet, Gettysburgians found another army advancing into their lives. The veteran Union cavalry men of Brigadier General John Buford's Division of the Army of the Potomac, dusty and weary from several weeks of continuous skirmishing with their Southern counterparts during their arduous trek northward, rode into Gettysburg searching for the elusive enemy which, at the time, was only eight miles distant.

As the twilight shaded into the moonlit darkness that 30 June, Buford and his Union troopers encamped northwest of town awaiting the first light of dawn to continue their search. However, only a blind man could not have seen the proverbial handwriting on the wall. According to several eyewitnesses, the mountain side eight miles west of town that night was dotted with numerous enemy camp fires.[4]

By first light of 1 July, Buford's cavalry pickets, some two miles west-northwest of the town, were challenged by Confederate infantry. Though neither Lee nor Union General George G. Meade had wanted to bring on a general engagement at this crossroads community, additional re-enforcements had been ordered into the fray by junior grade officers on both sides, expanding a small skirmish into a major battle. As the confrontation developed, Major General John F. Reynolds, commanding the Union 1st Corps, comprehending the delicate situation west of town, rushed elements of his command across open ground between the Emmitsburg Road and the Lutheran Seminary. Precious minutes were saved by cutting across the fields of the David McMillan and William Bliss Farms instead of following the roads north into town and then west to the area of the heaviest fighting.

Margaret McMillan, a granddaughter of David whose farm house was located a little over half a mile due south of the Seminary, recounted family oral tradition which described how David, as the battle developed west of

2

town, chopped down fence posts on his property to allow the Union troops to pass across his farm. When David's daughters, Laura and Carrie, saw:

> their father... with his axe, they took buckets and carried water for the soldiers who filled their canteens as they ran at double quick. Then Carrie, who [later in the afternoon?] was down at the spring, about 1/4 mile from the house, became alarmed [,she] started towards the Bliss house [situated about a half mile to the south-southeast] with a small basket of clothes which she had taken to wash.... When she remembered her sister, she asked several soldiers to tell Laura where she had gone. Meanwhile [as] Laura looked out of a window, and saw Carrie fleeing, ... she gathered up a few things, her father's Sunday suit, the family silver, and some articles, and left the house to join Carrie. They met at the Bliss house, but were obliged to leave there <u>with members of the Bliss family</u> very shortly afterward. They went across the fields [about two miles] to the [Jacob] Weikert home back [east] of Little Round Top where they stayed until after the battle was over.... [Emphasis added.][5]

Indeed, a Union soldier who fought at the Bliss Farm later wrote, "The people... evidently left in a hurry as they left the doors open, the table set, the beds made."[6]

By late afternoon the fortunes of the Union army had taken a turn for the worse. After twelve hours of battle two Union army corps had been mauled and forced back through town. Though the Confederates also suffered during the first day's battle, they had won a victory and occupied the town, but remnants of the two Union corps retreated only a short distance to two commanding heights south of town, Cemetery and Culp's Hills.

As for the Bliss family, their fortunes also had taken a turn for the worse during the night of 1st and the morning of the 2nd as the armies concentrated at Gettysburg. While the Union line eventually took the shape of a large fish hook as the Federal army's left flank was extended south along Cemetery Ridge, the Confederates lengthened their line along the ridge south of the Seminary which passed by the McMillan House. Consequently, the Bliss Farm buildings were situated dead center in the no man's land between the opposing forces.

William Bliss, the youngest of eleven surviving children of Dr. James and Hannah (Guild) Bliss, was born on 4 September 1799 at Rehoboth, Bristol County, Massachusetts. After marrying Adeline Carpenter on her

23rd birthday in 1823 and the birth of their daughter, William and his family moved circa 1828 from New England to a farm a mile southwest of the village of Warren Center in Warren Township, Bradford County, Pennsylvania. Remaining there for some five years and after the birth of their third daughter and a son, William and family continued their migration westward, and by 1835 they had settled on a new farm situated a mile southeast of Sinclairsville, Chautauqua County, New York where two more children were born. Residing there for nearly twenty-one years, the Bliss family suffered through several severe winters which probably contributed to the deaths of at least three of their six children (including his two sons). By the spring of 1857 William, Adeline and daughters Sarah and Frances moved to Gettysburg, for that April William officially purchased a small 53 acre farmstead west of the Emmitsburg Road. He bought an adjoining seven acres in 1858 (See Appendix F).

When the Blisses fled their home on the afternoon of 1 July, they little realized how the battle would affect their lives and the fate of a nation. As the battle lines formed on the 2nd, the Bliss property became tactically important due to the location of the farm buildings, topography, and ground cover.

The farmstead encompassed some sixty acres of the relatively flat land west of the Emmitsburg Road, and its large barn and house stood on a low, oblong hillock situated approximately 600 yards equidistant from the closest points on Cemetery and Seminary ridges. West of the farm buildings, the ground sloped very gently downward towards Seminary Ridge, dropping only five feet,[*] and about 100 yards short of its crest, it rose about fifteen feet at a moderate angle. In the opposite direction, the ground level dipped about eight feet over a distance of some thirty yards, between the house and barn and Stevens Run, a small stream (whose source was located on the Bliss Farm) which flowed northward into town. East of the stream the ground level sloped moderately, but unevenly, up to the crest of Cemetery Ridge, some fifty feet higher than the stream bed. Thus the hillock's summit was approximately at the same elevation as the crest of Seminary Ridge, but the crest of Cemetery Ridge was nearly forty feet higher. About 170 yards short of Cemetery Ridge's crest near Zeigler's Grove and the Abraham Brian farm buildings, and next to his tenant house and the residence of Emanuel Trostle, the Emmitsburg Road transected the area from north-northeast to south-southwest.

However, a key terrain feature was a broad, flat knoll, whose crest was situated about 450 yards to the east-northeast and about thirty feet higher

---

[*] Elevations are approximated by comparing contours on the 1867 Bachelder Maps of the battlefield with modern topographic maps.

than the Bliss buildings. Actually a spur of Cemetery Ridge, the knoll, averaging about 350 yards in width, extended slightly over a half mile to the north-northwest from Zeigler's Grove, but at a slightly lower elevation. Where the Emmitsburg Road cut through this feature, a man-made ditch was created which was up to three feet in depth.

The knoll created a blind spot north of the Bliss buildings. Soldiers in a position along the Stevens Run stream bed could not be seen from Cemetery Hill and Ridge, though they could be viewed from Seminary Ridge. Troops that advanced from positions on Cemetery Ridge could partially be observed from the Bliss Farm buildings and Seminary Ridge, but they could not be seen by troops in position along the stream bed. However, any soldiers operating along the Emmitsburg Road around the Brian tenant house were all but obscured from view from the Bliss buildings.

The lack of ground cover was critical because it afforded troops few places to hide from the "whizzing Minies" and the shot and shell of battle, except for the farmers' fences that crisscrossed the landscape and the relative safety of a ten-acre orchard whose eastern edge was located about fifty yards west of the farm structures. This orchard bisected the Bliss Farm and provided some cover across a 600 yard front from north to south.

The architecture of the farm buildings also was significant. Though the house was described in 1856 as a "double log and frame house, weatherboarded," twenty-eight years after the battle a former Connecticut soldier described it as:

> a mansion, a frame building, two stories in height. As it had a front of three rooms [bays] width, and two front doors, and there now [1891] remain two cellar excavations, with a thick earth wall between, over which it stood, indicating a length of about fifty feet.[7]

However, the real bastion was located about sixty yards to the south-southwest – the barn. The Connecticut soldier described the building as:

> almost a citadel in itself. It was an expensively and elaborately built structure... seventy-five feet long and thirty-three feet wide; its lower story, a basement [the stable area], ten feet high, constructed of stone and its upper part... of bricks. There was an over hang [forebay] ten feet wide along the entire front [east facade]... and the rear was banked to the first floor... furnishing a driveway for loads to that floor. There were five doors in the front wall of the basement and three windows in each end;

several long, narrow, vertical slits in the upper story and two rows of windows at each end....[8]

Hence, the Bliss Farmstead derived its tactical importance. Due to the structural strength of the barn and the house, these buildings along with the orchard, all situated on a slight hillock, provided the only significant cover for troops operating over 1,200 yards of relatively flat, open farm lands between the battle lines. The soldiers who could hold the house, barn, and orchard had an excellent view of the opponent's main position and fortifications, could monitor their opponents activities more accurately, and any sharpshooters stationed there could rain havoc on the enemy's troops all in relative safety.

However, the broad, flat knoll, though an asset for Federal troops, presented a tactical problem to the Confederates due to its location within rifle range of the Bliss Farm buildings and a portion of the orchard. As the day of 2 July wore on, Confederate commanders failed to analyze the problematic situation that developed at the Bliss Farm.

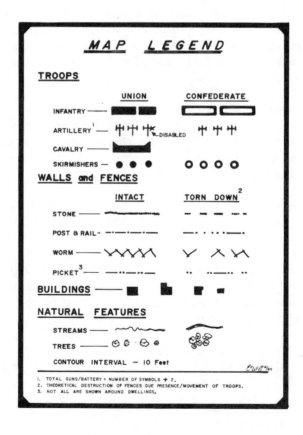

6

"... a citadel in itself."

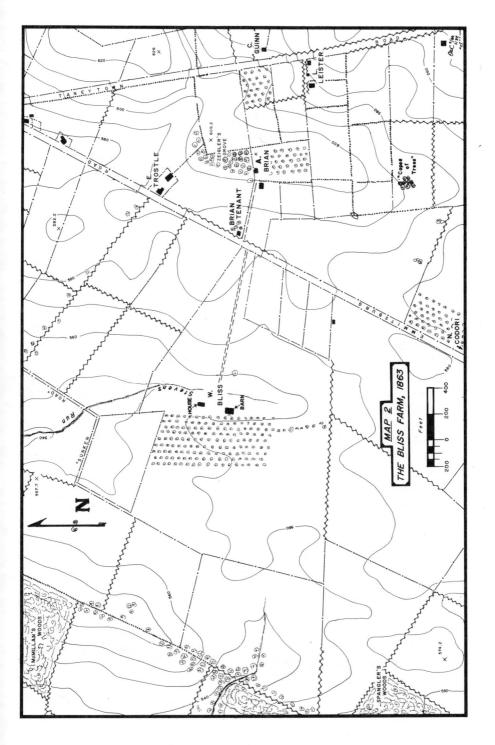

MAP 2

THE BLISS FARM, 1863

Chapter Two

"THAT BONE OF CONTENTION."

Before the sun rose the morning of 2 July, men, horses, and equipment were sent in motion that ultimately led to the destruction of the Bliss Farmstead.

West of Seminary Ridge, Lee prepared for his offensive operations. The Confederate troops that had suffered through the first day of Gettysburg were re-positioned in line of battle extending towards the west from a point near Culp's Hill, through the town to the Lutheran Seminary, and then south along the ridge. As fresh troops arrived, some of them were sent to the relief of the battered units while others were assigned positions in reserve. A few combat-weary commands, however, were selected for additional hazardous duties, and two such units were Lane's and Scales' brigades of Major General William Dorsey Pender's Division of Major General Ambrose P. Hill's Third Corps. These units that had participated in the final assaults on the Yankee positions at the Seminary the previous day.

Lane's Brigade of North Carolinians, composed of the 7th, 18th, 28th, 33rd, and 37th regiments, advanced up to the crest of Seminary Ridge where their line extended from a point near the Fairfield Road south to the McMillan Woods. There Lane was ordered to await further developments. Later, his troops were supported by Major General Henry Heth's divisional artillery battalion under the command of Lieutenant Colonel John J. Garnett.

James Henry Lane, described as "a two-fisted, vigorously human commander," was twenty-seven days short of his thirty-first birthday. A native of Matthews County, Virginia and a graduate of the Virginia Military Institute (VMI) and the University of Virginia (1857), Lane taught tactics at VMI and later served as professor of philosophy and instructor of military tactics at the North Carolina Military Institute.[9]

During two years of war, Lane had served as major of the 1st North Carolina Volunteers, colonel of the 28th North Carolina Regiment, and after the death of Brigadier General L. O'B. Branch on 17 September 1862 during the Battle of Antietam, he was elevated to brigade command. Based on his actions during the rear-guard engagement at Shepherdstown on that 20 September and "with the recommendations of Lee, 'Stonewall' Jackson, and A. P. Hill," Lane received his brigadier's star. He was later praised for his fighting ability at Fredericksburg despite the loss of more than 500 men defending the famous gap that was left in Jackson's line on the northern slopes of Prospect Hill. However, at Chancellorsville in May 1863 some of Lane's troops gained a dubious distinction – the men of the 18th North Carolina mistakenly shot and mortally wounded Jackson. Two months later, after forcing the Yankees before their gray tide at Gettysburg on 1 July, Lane was again preparing his North Carolinians for upcoming offensive operations.[10]

Near Lane's troops was the battered brigade of Brigadier General Alfred Scales, composed of the 13th, 16th, 22nd, 34th, and 38th North Carolina Regiments. Similar to Lane's command, these "Tar Heels" also had been engaged the previous day. However, Scales' Brigade had suffered far heavier casualties when they forced the remnants of the Union 1st Corps back from the Old Dorm of the Lutheran Seminary. By that evening, Scales, having been wounded, relinquished his command to Colonel William Lee J. Lowrance of the 34th North Carolina Regiment.[11]

Lowrance, a native of Iredell County and a teacher by trade, had enlisted near Salisbury during the summer of 1861 at the age of twenty-five, and by that mid-October he had been promoted to captain. Lowrance served with the 34th North Carolina Regiment throughout most of the campaigns of Lee's army and received his first wound at Gaines' Mill during the Seven Days Battles about Richmond. Like his brigade commander he, too, had been wounded on the first day at Gettysburg but was well enough to accept temporary command.[12]

In Lowrance's official report written a month after the battle, he described the condition of his troops after the first day's fighting. They were "depressed, dilapidated and almost unorganized", numbering about 500 effectives. In that condition, Colonel Lowrance and his men were to do more:

> At dawn... I was ordered to a position on the extreme right
> of and in line with the artillery..., and being an important
> point on the immediate right of our artillery, we its only
> guard and with no support, I considered it hazardous in the
> extreme.... So I threw out a strong line of skirmishers

> extending fully one-half mile to the right, reclining to the
> rear which was placed under the command of Lieutenant
> (A. J.) Brown of the 38th N. C. troops who most gallantly
> held the line against several strong skirmish lines thrown
> against him until 1 pm....[13]

Thus Scales' Brigade had been assigned a position at the extreme right flank of Lee's army. It was situated along the crest of Seminary Ridge south of McMillan Woods and to the right of Garnett's artillery. Lieutenant Brown's skirmish line probably extended south through the Bliss orchard curving westward to the vicinity of the northern edge of Spangler's Woods.

This assignment would not be the first time that Brown had been in charge of a skirmish line. A member of Company A of the 38th Regiment, the Sparta Band from Dublin County, 2nd Lieutenant Alsa J. Brown had been put in charge of sharpshooters for several days during the Battle of Chancellorsville, and was praised in Pender's official report on that battle. Lieutenant Brown was:

> a young man who deserves promotion. He kept his
> skirmishers as close to the enemy breastworks... as to pick
> off the artillery horses, men working on their trenches, and
> anyone seen noted. He drove in other skirmishers on all
> occasions.[14]

At Gettysburg, Brown was to have a difficult time with Yankee pickets.

Meanwhile, across the fields some two miles to the southeast, near the eastern slopes of the Round Tops, men of the 3rd Division, commanded by Brigadier General Alexander Hays, of Major General Winfield S. Hancock's 2nd Corps of the Army of the Potomac, were stirring after their all too brief rest. Similar to Lane, Hays was barely a week away from a birthday, his forty-fourth. A native of Franklin, Venango County, Pennsylvania, he graduated from West Point in 1842, twentieth in his class. Like many future Civil War generals, he had fought during the War with Mexico and had received a brevet for gallantry. Upon his return he resigned his commission to seek a career in the private sector. At the onset of the Southern Rebellion, Hays re-enlisted in the regular army and briefly served as a captain in the 16th U. S. Infantry before receiving his commission as colonel of the 63rd Pennsylvania Volunteer Regiment in October 1861. Due to his conspicuous service during the Seven Days Battles and at Second Bull Run, where he fell seriously wounded, he was promoted to brigadier general in the fall of 1862. However, Hays required nearly ten months to recuperate from his wounds, convalescing at Washington, D. C.. Only three days before the opening shots were fired at Gettysburg, he received command of the 3rd Division of the 2nd Corps composed of two battle-weary brigades and a third which had been organized only two days earlier.[15]

Hays' 1st Brigade, composed of the 14th Indiana, 4th and 8th Ohio, and the 7th West Virginia Regiments, was commanded by a native Marylander. Samuel Spriggs Carroll was born in the early fall of 1832 at Takoma Park, Montgomery County just outside of the District of Columbia. As a member of the West Point Class of 1856, he graduated towards the bottom of his class, and his early military career was spent on frontier duty followed by a stint as quartermaster at his alma mater. After the outbreak of the Civil War, Carroll was appointed colonel of the 8th Ohio Volunteers in December 1861.[16]

Carroll joined his new command near Romney in mountainous wilds of what would become part of West Virginia. Carroll and his men of the 8th Ohio spent the first quarter of the new year guarding the line of the Baltimore and Ohio Railroad and protecting the various locks along the upper sections of the Chesapeake and Ohio Canal along the Potomac. That March, Carroll and his Buckeyes were assigned to Shields' Division, spending most of the spring chasing and being chased by Stonewall Jackson during the Valley Campaign of 1862. By the latter part of June, Carroll and the 8th Ohio were shipped to Harrison's Landing, Virginia, arriving in time to witness the final Confederate attacks at Malvern Hill. During the Second Manassas Campaign, Carroll and his men were shipped back to the Union capital and assigned to Kimble's Independent Brigade of the 2nd Corps, and from that time Carroll and the 8th Ohio were involved in all of the major campaigns of the Army of the Potomac.[17]

The 2nd Brigade of Hays' Division, comprised of the 14th Connecticut, 1st Delaware, 12th New Jersey and 108th New York Regiments and the 10th New York Battalion, was commanded by an Irishman. Thomas A. Smyth, born on Christmas day 1832 at Ballyhooly, Cork, Ireland, emigrated to the United States in 1854 and settled in Philadelphia before establishing "a business in carving." About a year later, Smyth, among others, joined William Walker in his infamous expedition to Nicaragua. After Walker was ousted from power, Smyth returned to the United States and settled in Wilmington, Delaware where he became a coach maker.[18]

However, Smyth's new profession was short-lived, for with the outbreak of hostilities in April 1861, Smyth voluntarily recruited a company of men that became part of the all-Irish 24th Pennsylvania Volunteers, whose three-month stint ended about the time of the First Battle at Manassas. After the expiration of his term of service, Smyth received the appointment as major of the 1st Delaware Volunteers in the fall of 1861.[19]

11

From Wilmington, Smyth and his new regiment were sent to Fort Monroe at Hampton Roads, Virginia where they witnessed the history-making naval engagement between the two iron-clads, the U. S. S. *Monitor* and the C. S. S. *Virginia.* However, by the fall of 1862 Union General George B. McClellan's army had been decisively outmaneuvered and defeated east of Richmond, and a secondary Federal force under General John Pope had suffered the same fate on the old battlefield near Manassas Junction, both engagements executed by Lee and his newly-named Army of Northern Virginia. With Lee's Southern army near Washington, Federal troops, including the 1st Delaware, were returned to the nation's capital and rejoined the Army of the Potomac, once again with McClellan at the helm. At Antietam, like many Federal regiments that had just been assigned to the army, Smyth and the 1st Delaware "saw the elephant" (baptism of fire) for the first time. During the battle, the 1st Delaware lost a third of its complement as casualties by the banks of the infamous "Bloody Lane." Smyth's performance resulted in his promotion to colonel of the regiment, and after Chancellorsville, he was assigned the command of the 2nd Brigade though he would have to wait over a year to receive his brigadier's star.[20]

Lastly, commanding the newly-organized 3rd Brigade of Hays' Division was Colonel Charles Lamb Willard, a native of New York City born in August 1827. Though he wanted to continue the military traditions of his mother's family by attending West Point, his parents thought it would be best for the young man to become a "practical businessman." As a result he was sent to live with a relative in Ohio. But at the onset of the Mexican War, young Willard enlisted in the 15th Ohio Volunteers, and like several future Civil War officers, he scaled the walls of Chapultepec Castle. Willard was breveted 2nd Lieutenant in the 8th United States Infantry in late June 1848, and a month later he was commissioned in the regular army as a 2nd Lieutenant in that regiment.[21]

Willard served "almost continuously" on the frontier in Texas and in the New Mexico Territory after the Mexican War. In 1860, he was granted a leave of absence and returned to the East; shortly afterward his regiment was captured in Texas at the outbreak of hostilities. Being a soldier without a command, Willard was promoted to Captain and appointed Assistant Adjutant-General on Major General John E. Wool's staff. After his unit's exchange, Willard rejoined his regiment which was then undergoing reorganization at Newport Barracks, Kentucky.[22]

Willard served in the Regulars through the Peninsula Campaign in 1862. On his thirty-fifth birthday (15 August) he was promoted to colonel and given the command of a newly-formed volunteer unit, the 125th New York Regiment. However, his green troops along with two other newly-formed New York units, the 111th and 126th, and the veterans of the 39th

New York were captured by Stonewall Jackson at Harpers Ferry during Lee's Maryland Campaign. The New Yorkers, after spending several months at Camp Douglas near Chicago, were exchanged, shipped back east, and by Chirstmas 1862 were assigned to tedious duties in and about the defenses of Washington. Six months later, on 26 June 1863, Colonel Willard was given the command of a newly-organized brigade, composed of the 39th, 111th, his 125th, and the 126th New York Regiments, which was assigned to Hays' 3rd Division and ordered to join the Army of the Potomac in the field.[23]

On 1 July, as the men of the Union 1st and 11th Corps desperately tried to maintain their positions west and north of Gettysburg, Hays' 3rd Division had trod some fifteen foot-sore miles from Uniontown, Maryland and bivouacked late that evening. By first light of 2 July the division was again on the road and briskly marched towards Gettysburg, and upon reaching the vicinity of Meade's headquarters at the Lydia Leister farmstead, it was deployed. Hays was ordered to post his men to the left of the cemetery; thus his line extended about 600 yards along Cemetery Ridge from Cemetery Hill to a point several yards short of an umbrella-shaped copse of trees. His command relieved the men of Robinson's Division of the 1st Corps, who had suffered severely during the previous day's fighting.[24]

As his troops arrived near Meade's headquarters, Smyth's Brigade was apparently at the head of the column. As Smyth's men left the road, he positioned most of his regiments in the vicinity of Zeigler's Grove. A picket detail was needed, so Smyth assigned his old regiment to the task. According to 1st Lieutenant John Louis Brady of Company E, "the regiment was sent forward and at once deployed as skirmishers, with Lieutenant Colonel E[dward] P. Harris of the 1st Delaware in command of the line." Thus, these 250 veterans were to be the first Union challengers for the right to occupy the Bliss buildings.[25]

Brady probably would have felt right at home with the Scots-Irish residents of Adams County. Born in the summer of 1839 in the Old Dominion State, Brady was the son of an Irish father and a Scottish mother. In his senior years, Brady's demeanor was described as "standing at the very top of...citizenship." According to the 1860 Census, Brady resided in Wilmington and listed his occupation as that of a "Captain." However, a year later, he enrolled in the 1st Delaware and was appointed as a sergeant. Prior to his unit's return to Washington after the Seven Days Battles, he was promoted to first sergeant. Additional responsibilities followed quickly. On 6 January 1863, eleven days after Brady received the stripes of sergeant-major, he was promoted to 2nd Lieutenant of Company D. On 7 February, he was assigned as 1st Lieutenant of Company E.[26]

"Shortly after daylight," as Brady recalled, the men were deployed and advanced towards the Bliss buildings under a "brisk fire," probably from Scales' and Lane's pickets. Lieutenant Brown's outnumbered North Carolina skirmishers apparently were forced back through the Bliss orchard since the buildings were secured by the men of the 1st Delaware. Lieutenant Colonel Harris divided his command into two battalions. The "left wing", which included Brady's Company E, extended south from the barn into a wheat field. The "right wing" extended some distance to the north into that part of Bliss' orchard consisting of peach trees. The regimental command post was established in the barn. Brady recalled "remaining under a rattling fire from the enemy which was repaid with interest until about 8 o'clock AM," when the re-enforced enemy skirmishers counter-attacked. As pressure came to bear on the advanced skirmish line of the 1st Delaware, their right wing was slowly forced back and driven, in part, towards the Bliss buildings. As Brady termed it, they were under a "galling fire of a largely superior force."[27]

During this onslaught, Brady discussed the deteriorating situation on the right flank with his company commander, Captain Martin W. B. Ellegood. After a "brief but hurried" consultation with him, Brady searched for his regiment's commander and found Harris "in the basement of the barn." Brady reported the serious situation developing on the right flank:

> Whereupon, he [Harris] after carefully venturing from his safe retreat and taking a very hasty glance over the situation, turned and _fled_ precipitously towards our main line, leaving that portion of the field, in the immediate charge of [1st] Lieutenant [Charles B.] Tanner [of Company D] and myself.[28]

As interpreted by Brady, the deteriorating situation on the skirmish line was too much for the twenty-four year old commander of the Delawarians. Born near Georgetown, Delaware, Harris enlisted in the army in July 1861 and was mustered in as captain of Company E. However, he did not "see the elephant" at Antietam. During the move from Virginia to Washington in the late summer of 1862, Harris was detached and assigned as recruitment officer in his home town. Following the blood bath near Sharpsburg, Maryland, Harris rejoined the 1st Delaware and served as an interim commander for a month. At Fredericksburg in December 1862, he not only received his baptism of fire but received a "red badge of courage" in the process. By mid-morning of 2 July, according to Brady, Harris' instinct to survive negated his duty to his comrades.[29] Whatever the reasons were for Harris' actions, they had negative results, and as Harris

14

"That bone of contention."

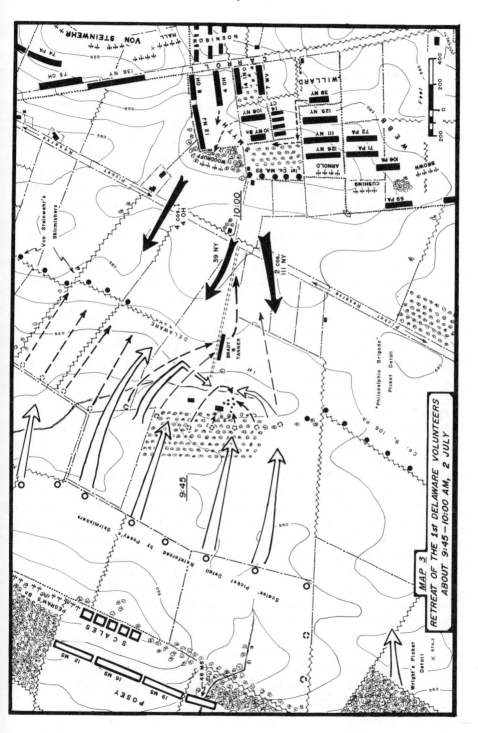

MAP 3

RETREAT OF THE *1st* DELAWARE VOLUNTEERS
ABOUT 9:45–10:00 AM, 2 JULY

15

dashed towards the rear, the fate of the 1st Delaware was left in the hands of two junior-grade officers.

Brady's compatriot on the skirmish line was twenty-one year old Charles B. Tanner, a native of Wilmington, Delaware. At Antietam nine months earlier, as his unit battled with the Confederate troops in "Bloody Lane," Tanner had volunteered to retrieve the regimental colors which laid amongst the bodies of the color guard some fifty yards away. As the Delawarians laid down a covering fire, Tanner dashed forward to within twenty yards of the enemy lines and secured the flags. However, for his deed, Tanner was wounded three times, but apparently two of them must have been minor wounds; his pension records indicate that only one wound was treated – in the fleshy part of his left forearm. Twenty-seven years later, Tanner received the Medal of Honor for his actions on 17 September 1862.[30]

After Harris left the picket line, the situation there deteriorated at an accelerating rate. The right wing was being "sorely pressed by an overwhelming force in its front." Seeing the right flank disintegrating before their eyes, the two lieutenants moved towards the right and managed to rally "a few remaining men at hand into line along the southern side" of a fence which paralleled the farm lane running from the Bliss buildings to the Emmitsburg Road. There, just east of the barn, the men fired a "few well directed shots" at the advancing enemy which forced the Confederates to move obliquely to their right and towards the Bliss barn. This movement split the two wings of the 1st Delaware. Cut off from the rest of the regiment and now missing Tanner who had left the field, hit in his right wrist[31] by a "pistol ball," Brady had no other alternative but to fall back to Cemetery Ridge and the safety of the main Union line.[32]

As the right of the 1st Delaware melted away, the left wing south of the barn was not faring any better. With the deteriorating situation, these Delawarians attempted to refuse their right flank to protect the rest of the battalion from an enfilade coming from the area just east of the barn. However, it was too late – the Confederates, who had fired upon Brady and Tanner's little band, had swung around the front of the barn, and together with the Southerners advancing from the west, they formed a "cordon" around some of the Union skirmishers. Cut off from the main body of their regiment, most of the left wing (except possibly Company K on the extreme left) managed to retire from the field. However;

> Here it was that Captain... Ellegood yielded up his young life... and here too it was that my old friend Captain [Ezechiel C.] Alexander [of Company H] together with some of the 'Boys'... [were captured].[33]

16

Like Tanner, Captain Alexander was no stranger to combat. At the age of twenty-three he had been wounded during each of the three prior engagements to Gettysburg, and he, too, had been very fortunate. At Fredericksburg, he had been shot through the body. The projectile struck his right shoulder, passed below the collar bone, and exited below his right shoulder blade. Apparently the bullet did not tear through any vital parts for Ezechiel had recuperated sufficiently to return to his unit. He was promoted to 1st Lieutenant and was wounded at Chancellorsville the following May.[34]

One of the more tragic stories, however, was the loss of Captain Ellegood. Born at Georgetown, Delaware in 1840, the only son of six children, Martin moved with his parents to Philadelphia. There he worked for a lawyer some two years and as a clerk selling "Notions" for a Mr. Ott at 4th and Market Streets. During the spring of 1861, Martin visited his home town and volunteered his services to the Union. According to pension records, young Ellegood had been unemployed six months prior to his enlistment, and was considered to be unskilled in any trade. After his muster into service his mother, Elizabeth, died of consumption in November 1861 at Philadelphia.[35]

From the field, "Mart" (as he was called by family members) wrote home on a regular basis. In a letter to his sister Julia dated 2 March 1863, Mart reminisced about the good old days, lamented the loss of his mother, and reflected on the horrors of war:

> Tis a beautiful moonlight night. Just such a one as one loves to see. It reminds me of the old times of those days when in the innocence of childhood I have viewed the scene from my mother's side. Those scenes come fresh to my mind. But they have past – past! Oh! What changes! It makes me sad to think of them, yet the remembrances do me good. I love to dwell on those days. ...I hear the violin [,] one crowd is having a good old time. Then I hear the drum corps singing a song far away off[.] Some are singing a hymn, whilst a few are standing in groups talking about one thing and then another. If I was to go in some tents I would find some doing as I am, others reading, and not a few playing cards. Such is the picture of camplife by the moonlight.[36]

Mart must have been a fine, responsible son. Besides commanding a company of men, Martin worried about his kin in Philadelphia. Apparently, his father was having financial difficulties for Mart sent him as much as $100 of his pay. However, sister Julia was a spendthrift. Shortly before the commencement of the Gettysburg Campaign, Martin wrote to someone named "Nat," expressing his concern over his father working, the extravagance of his sister Julia, and their aloofness towards his hardships. Mart felt that:

> Fine clothes and good furniture is Julia's Gods. ...There is no telling how long I will be able to help the family. I think so far I have done my duty. But I might get killed, or which is worse, wounded for life, and I think I ought to save something whilst I have a chance. ... [Emphasis added][37]

Apparently Julia had purchased a new carpet, and the extravagance was too much for the young captain for Martin continued:

> when they think that many a night I have to lay upon the cold ground with nothing but the canopy of the heavens to cover me. Many nights whilst they are comfortably sleeping in their warm beds, I am exposed to the pelting rain, wet to the skin. It appears to me, when they are so extravagant, they have no feelings for me.[38]

Only a month later, Captain Ellegood's worst fears had been realized – he fell mortally wounded near the Bliss barn – lingering four days before passing away on 6 July at one of the many field hospitals that dotted the Gettysburg landscape. His body was returned to Delaware and interred in the St. Paul's Protestant Episcopal Church graveyard in Georgetown. The epitaph chiseled upon his stone undoubtedly was added after Lincoln's immortal Gettysburg Address, for it read, "One of the number who gave his life that his country might live."[39]

With the defeat of the Delawarians about 10:00 AM, Hays' Division front was laid bare by the Southern hosts, and the Bliss barn, "that bone of contention," was occupied by soldiers dressed in butternut and gray. This development forced General Hays to perform a juggling act on the crest of Cemetery Ridge.[40] Earlier, fresh troops of Carroll's and Willard's Brigades along with the 2nd Corps artillery had filed off the Taneytown Road and moved into position – the artillery to the front with the infantry in reserve. As the situation on the skirmish line deteriorated, elements of these commands were assigned the task to re-establish Hays' picket line west of the Emmitsburg Road.

One of the first details sent belatedly to the aid of the 1st Delaware, were men of the 4th Ohio Volunteers, part of Carroll's Brigade, commanded by twenty-nine year-old Lieutenant Colonel Leonard W. Carpenter. Born at Indiana, Pennsylvania, Carpenter enlisted in the 4th Ohio while he was attending medical school in Mt. Vernon, Ohio.[41] Mt. Vernon was the home town of a composer of minstrel tunes, Daniel Decatur Emmett, whose most famous composition was "I wish I was in Dixie's Land." However, the lieutenant colonel had more pressing matters on his mind than the refrain of that then-popular Southern tune. According to Carpenter in his after-action report, "At 9:30 AM I received orders to advance four companies... under the command of Major [Gordon A.] Stewart."[42] This movement was corroborated by Private William Kepler of Company D, 4th Ohio who recalled that elements of his regiment were sent to the skirmish line "near the Emmitsburg Road" by order of Colonel Carroll along with two other companies.[43] Those other two companies were part of the 111th New York Regiment of Willard's Brigade. Colonel Clinton D. McDougall, commander of the 111th, wrote that "two companies were detailed as skirmishers..." soon after the New Yorkers had arrived on the crest of the ridge near the Brian farm buildings.[44]

Lastly, a short time later, the 39th New York Regiment, the famous "Garibaldi Guard," was sent forward deploying "in front of and to the right of the [Bliss] barn."[45] The Garibaldi Guard, named after the famous contemporary Italian patriot, Giuseppe Garibaldi, had a definite international air. The unit was originally composed of Germans, Hungarians, Swiss, French, Spanish and Portuguese emigrants, and their uniforms were patterned after the Italian Light Infantry or "Bersaglieri" of the era.[46] The men of the 39th had "seen the elephant" at 1st Bull Run and were involved in the hunt for Stonewall Jackson in the Shenandoah Valley. After their capture at Harpers Ferry in September 1862, their exchange, and their assignment to help defend Washington, the Garibaldi Guard was consolidated into four companies and assigned to Willard's Brigade.[47]

Though the situation was a bit hectic in the vicinity of Zeigler's Grove during the forenoon of 2 July, General Hays had managed to stabilize the situation on his skirmish line. As the bulk of the 1st Delaware retreated, the Confederates were faced with ten fresh companies of enemy infantry: four each from the Garibaldi Guard and the 4th Ohio, and two from the 111th New York.

Across the fields to the west about mid-morning, the Confederate skirmishers of Scales' and Lane's Brigades, who had been forced back from the Bliss Farm buildings by the advance of the 1st Delaware, had been re-enforced by pickets from Major General Richard H. Anderson's Division of A. P. Hill's Corps. Anderson had been ordered to extend the Confederate line south along Seminary Ridge from the vicinity of the McMillan House through Spangler's Woods. As the bulk of Anderson's troops settled into position, his skirmishers advanced forward and assisted in the counterattack on the Bliss buildings about 9:30-10:00 AM.

Richard Heron "Fighting Dick" Anderson was born in the fall of 1821 into the wealthy plantation society, at the family home at Statesborough, South Carolina. He was said to have had "a taste for the military." At the age of seventeen, Dick disappointed his father by electing to attend the United States Military Academy. Entering West Point in 1838, he made several lasting friendships with future allies Daniel Harvey Hill and James Longstreet and future antagonists John Pope and Abner Doubleday. After graduating fortieth in his class in 1842, Dick Anderson distinguished himself during the Mexican War and was breveted 1st Lieutenant for "gallantry and meritorious conduct."[48] With the close of hostilities Anderson remained in the army and was reassigned to Carlisle Barracks (located thirty miles north of Gettysburg). There he established family ties, meeting and marrying Sarah Gibson, the daughter of the Chief Justice of the Pennsylvania Supreme Court. Shortly thereafter, Anderson was transferred, serving out west in Texas and Utah where he assisted in the suppression of the Mormons.[49]

With South Carolina's secession Anderson returned to his native state in March 1861 and was appointed colonel of the 1st South Carolina Regular Regiment which was serving in Charleston during the bombardment of Fort Sumter. Later, he was assigned to command the Charleston forces when General P. G. T. Beauregard was transferred to Richmond that summer. With Anderson's promotion to brigadier, he was assigned to General Braxton Bragg's command at Pensacola, Florida. Running afoul with Bragg nearly ended Anderson's career; he was transferred to Richmond and given a command in Longstreet's Division. During successive campaigns of Lee's Army of Northern Virginia, Anderson distinguished himself, receiving praise from his superiors, and he was eventually promoted to divisional command.[50]

A major Confederate player in the Bliss Farm struggle commanded a brigade under Anderson. It consisted of the 12th, 16th, 19th and 48th Mississippi Regiments and it was in the van of Anderson's column that morning. Brigadier General Carnot Posey was born in August 1818 in rural Wilkinson County, Mississippi, south of Natchez; attended school in Jackson, Louisiana; and later graduated from the University of Virginia with a law degree. Upon his return to Wilkinson County, Carnot continued life as a planter, augmenting his revenues with his law practice at Woodville. During the Mexican War, Posey joined Colonel Jefferson Davis' Mississippi Rifles in 1846 (where he eventually attained the rank of 1st Lieutenant) and participated in the Battle at Buena Vista where he was wounded. After the war, during the Buchanan Administration, Posey served as the United States District Attorney for southern Mississippi.[51]

With the outbreak of the Civil War, Posey raised a company of men, the Wilkinson Rifles, which was mustered in at Cornith and re-designated as Company B of the 16th Mississippi Volunteers. Carnot served honorably during the first fourteen months of the war; both he and R. H. Anderson were praised for their conduct at Manassas and Antietam. Another brigadier wrote in his report of actions at Kelly's Ford that "much credit is due to Colonel Posey... for the handsome manner in which [his troops] repelled the attack of Federal cavalry."[52] In November, 1862, Posey was promoted to brigadier general, and as a brigade commander at Chancellorsville he "conducted himself with gallantry for which he had always been distinguished."[53] Three months later, at Gettysburg, Posey and his men had another opportunity to repel the Federals.

As the Mississippians arrived on the Confederate right flank to support Scales' North Carolinians, Posey:

> placed [his men] in a position... in rear of Major [William J.] Pegram's [battalion, of A. P. Hill's reserve] artillery in an open field with woods on my right and my left [the area between McMillan and Spangler's woods].

A short time later, at least Company C of the 16th Mississippi Regiment and Lieutenant C. W. Burrage and some men of the 19th Mississippi Regiment were detailed as skirmishers.[54]

Documentation suggests that as the men of Lane's and Scales' picket detail hammered away at the 1st Delaware, Posey's skirmishers poured into the fray. With additional men on the skirmish line by, and to the north of, the Bliss buildings, the gray line surged forward, turned the right of the Delawarians and forced Brady and his small force back towards Cemetery Ridge. Concurrently, the additional pressure on the left of the 1st Delaware from the west, and the Confederate encircling movement around the Bliss barn snared Captain Alexander and some of the "Boys." However, a short time later General Hays managed to replace the defeated Federal skirmishers and, in turn, by about 10:00 AM they forced the Confederates away from the Bliss buildings and back through the orchard.

However, an hour later, additional Southern troops maneuvered into position on Seminary Ridge. By 11:00 AM the brigades of Brigadier Generals William "Scrappy Billy" Mahone and Ambrose R. Wright of Anderson's Division arrived. Wright's command marched to the vicinity of Spangler's Woods on Posey's right and Mahone's Brigade assumed a position in reserve somewhere in the vicinity of the southwest corner of McMillan Woods. However, both Wright and Mahone deployed skirmishers to their respective fronts, thereby re-enforcing the picket lines in the vicinity of the Bliss Farm. To the north, elements of Brigadier General Edward L. Thomas' Brigade of Pender's Division also had been deployed to assist the pickets of Lane's command. Second Lieutenant Draughton S. Haynes, commanding Company I, 49th Georgia Regiment, wrote in his diary that the "skirmishing was very heavy in front, several of my regiment having been wounded."[55] This increased activity along the Confederate lines did not go unnoticed on Cemetery Ridge.

Around 11 A.M. General Hays noticed the re-enforced gray skirmish line beginning to pressure the Union pickets near the Bliss Farm. According to one soldier:

> a lively skirmish took place, and the enemy's reinforcements... coming from the northwest through the orchard close to the barn, began to drive back the 39th New York.

Again, Hays was on top of the situation. The general and his adjutant, attempting to ascertain the condition of his skirmish line:

> dashed down on horseback to the line and rode back again unharmed. Major [Hugo] Hildebrand [commanding the 39th] who was also on horseback was severely wounded in the foot.[56]

With the situation at the Bliss Farmstead deteriorating once more, Hays began to assemble troops to bolster his picket line. Near the Brian House, Hays' divisional headquarters, three companies of the 125th New York Regiment under the command of Captain Charles M. Wheeler[57] were readied to be sent to the front. Nearby, men of the 12th New Jersey Regiment, which had been re-positioned on the battle line on Cemetery Ridge, also were to assist in this latest emergency. According to one officer, the Jerseymen, who had been "... placed in a position in rear of the cemetery, facing town [or north]..." earlier that morning, were ordered to change position near noon. The 12th was shifted to the left some 200 yards taking a new position with their right flank resting very near the Brian "house,"[58] and once this movement was completed, the men of Company I prepared for picket duty. Lastly, Lieutenant Colonel Harris and some men of the 1st Delaware, reorganized after their earlier engagement, prepared to advance once again.[59]

To add to the confusion, the boom of artillery joined the chorus of rifle fire. Earlier that morning, Captain John G. Hazard, commanding the 2nd Corps artillery, had deployed his five batteries along the crest of Cemetery Ridge. Three of these were among the regiments of Hays' command. Battery I, 1st United States Artillery commanded by 1st Lieutenant George A. Woodruff, was posted amongst the trees of Zeigler's Grove while Battery A, 1st Rhode Island Light Artillery under Captain William A. Arnold, was unlimbered on Hays' left flank, about 100 yards north of the Copse of Trees. Adjacent to Arnold's left was Battery A, 4th United States Artillery commanded by 1st Lieutenant Alonzo Cushing. As these three Union batteries opened fire, Hays was completing the assemblage of the infantry that was to replace the men of the 39th New York.

Though the situation was confused in the vicinity of Zeigler's Grove, as the men of the Garibaldi Guard fell back, fresh troops were substituted – a conglomeration composed of the three companies of the 125th New York, Company I of the 12th New Jersey, and remnants of the 1st Delaware, all under the command of Lieutenant Colonel Harris.[60] Nearby, 2nd Lieutenant Theron E. Parsons (Company D, 108th New York), an aide-de-camp to Colonel Smyth, recorded in his diary that he had:

> expected to move down and attack the enemy, but it was merely a detail of the First Delaware as skirmishers. They are out now and we can hear them yell as they run through the fields after the graybacks. The batteries in our front are dropping their shells among the Rebels with what effects we cannot tell.

This artillery fire was kept up at intervals throughout the day.[61]

As for the men of the 39th New York, they had performed admirably, but not without loss. During the late morning, "the Garibaldis lost 28 killed and wounded" including 2nd Lieutenant Adolphus Wagner of Company C, who fell mortally wounded.[62]

To the west across the mile-wide plain, apparently the Confederates were not too concerned about the turn of events on their skirmish line shortly after the noon hour. Earlier Lieutenant Garnett had:

> received an order to send all my rifles [rifled cannon] to a position immediately opposite Cemetery Hill and to the right [south] of the Fairfield Turnpike. I accordingly dispatched Major [Charles] Richardson with nine rifled pieces of the battalion to the hill indicated [vicinity of the McMillan house and woods] where they remained in

position until the following morning. At 3 PM... these pieces open fire.[63]

Further along the line, Major William T. Poague's battalion, Pender's divisional artillery, arrived in the vicinity of McMillan Woods "about 11 o'clock, [but] took no part in the engagement" of 2 July. Colonel R. Lindsey Walker, commander of the Artillery Reserve of A. P. Hill's Corps, simply stated in his official report that his batteries opened "at intervals" during the day. Lastly, Major John Lane commanding the Sumter (Georgia) Artillery, moved Anderson's divisional artillery battalion into position with his men enduring the shelling of some "Napoleon guns" (possibly including Woodruff's guns), but he did not indicate whether his guns responded to the Union challenge.[64]

As for the Confederate infantry, their brigade commanders took the loss of the Bliss buildings in stride. McGowen's Brigade of Pender's Division, commanded by Colonel Abner Perrin, moved into:

> position in rear of some artillery [probably Garnett's nine rifled pieces] as a support, [where they] were exposed to and suffered a small loss from the enemy's shells.[65]

However, no general advance was made. A soldier in Company B, 16th Mississippi, wrote in his diary that:

> Around 1 P. M. we relieved Scales Brigade, moving forward to knock the boards off a fence that stood in our front.[66]

Moreover, after the recall of Scales' skirmishers, his entire command (500 men less casualties) pulled out of line and rejoined Pender's Division north of McMillan Woods.

Thus after seven hours of see-saw fighting around the Bliss property, a lull occurred in the action with the Federals retaining possession of the farm buildings. However, the early afternoon lull was deceiving.

Chapter Three

Afternoon and Evening, 2 July 1863
"YES SIR, THE 12TH WILL DO IT!"
"TRUE TO THEIR TRUST"

By late morning, Lee had finalized his plans for the day's offensive operations which he generally outlined in his official report dated January 1864:

> It was determined to make the principal attack upon the enemy's left.... [Lieutenant General James] Longstreet was directed to place the divisions of McLaws and Hood on the right of Hill, partially enveloping the enemy's left, which he was to drive in.
>
> General Hill was ordered to threaten the enemy's center, to prevent re-enforcements being drawn to either wing, and co-operate with his right division [R. H. Anderson's] in Longstreet's attack.
>
> General [Richard S.] Ewell [commanding the Second Corps] was instructed to make a simultaneous demonstration upon the enemy's right, to be converted into a real attack should opportunity offer.[67]

In reality Lee's plan was too complicated to coordinate and execute under the existing circumstances, and several inherent problems within the Confederate army had a direct bearing on the battle and the fighting for the Bliss Farmstead.

By the summer of 1863, the war had exacted a heavy toll on the Confederate high command with key positions needing to be filled. Lee was aware that the organization of the Army of Northern Virginia had to undergo a major reshuffling after the death of Stonewall Jackson that spring. However, with the supply of highly qualified officers dwindling, Lee also realized that his two corps had become too large for effective and smooth combat operations, especially in mountainous or wooded terrain. Thus, before the Gettysburg Campaign, Lee reorganized his army, creating a third corps and promoting Hill and Ewell to corps command. However, the reorganization resulted in the break up of several effective combat entities, thereby altering an *esprit de corps* that had been forged during two years of hard campaigning.

Of the utmost importance, the army needed a more efficient staff system. Regardless of the caliber of combat officers, if the transmission and interpretation of Lee's strategy was not accurately communicated to the combat officers down the chain of command, Lee's improvements would come to naught. Though he improved the Army of Northern Virginia's combat readiness, Lee neglected to overhaul the system by which the various elements of the army communicated. Indeed, Lee's staff system has been described as "slovenly" and it plagued the high command during the entire Gettysburg Campaign.[68]

Lastly, the unpredictability of the enemy was significant. In previous engagements, Lee had been faced with opponents whom he had known personally prior to the Civil War. However, Lee probably never met Major General Daniel E. Sickles, the commander of the Union 3rd Corps, one of those unpredictable, crafty, Tammany Hall politicians from New York City. It was Sickles and his command that was placed towards the Union left flank, the main focus of Confederate attacks.

As Lee's offensive operations were implemented during the noon hour that 2 July, his plans began to unravel due to unanticipated variables that reality had factored into his strategy formula. After the see-saw fighting at the Bliss Farm waned about 1:00 PM, Longstreet, who had spent most of the late morning and early afternoon marching and counter-marching his troops behind Seminary Ridge, expended an exorbitant amount of daylight marching to the southern section of Seminary (Warfield) Ridge. As the major fighting developed in the late afternoon, Lee's plan was continually modified, compensating for actual battlefield conditions. The continuing struggle for the Bliss Farm was one of those modulating factors.

Sometime after 3:00 PM, Longstreet's artillery opened fire on the Union left flank, signaling the beginning of the Confederate attacks which were made "en echelon." Consequently, the situation began to heat up around the Bliss property. Garnett's nine rifled pieces, among others, began to shell the Union forces in the area of Zeigler's Grove and Cemetery Hill, and the gray infantrymen likewise increased their pressure on the skirmish line.

When taken at face value, the official reports that have survived, submitted by Posey and the commanding officer of the 19th Mississippi, tend to contradict each other regarding the events of the afternoon of 2 July. Posey's sequence does not mesh with that of his subordinate. But, if one realizes that, theoretically, Posey prepared his report after reviewing those of his subordinates and that Posey, possibly in his haste, placed certain occurrences out of proper sequence, a different chain of events emerges which is not immediately evident in the surviving reports. When compared with several official documents and personal accounts of their Federal counterparts, the new sequence is corroborated. The series of events that occurred on the Bliss Farm following the initiation of Longstreet's attack altered the outcome of the day's engagement.

Near McMillan Woods, Posey was in a quandary. In his official report he wrote, "In the afternoon, I received an order to advance after General Wright who was posted [in Spangler's Woods]" – the en echelon plan. Before Wright's Brigade advanced, however, Posey received another order "from the Major General [Anderson] through his aide-de-camp, Captain (S[amuel] D.) Shannon," and Posey, interpreting it, advanced "but two of my regiments [the 19th and 48th Mississippi] and deployed them closely as skirmishers."[69]

Colonel Nathaniel H. Harris, commanding the 19th Mississippi, was one of the rising stars of the Army of Northern Virginia. Born in August 1834 in the bustling Mississippi River town of Natchez, Harris graduated from the University of Louisiana (now Tulane) and later practiced law in Vicksburg until the commencement of the Civil War. During May 1861 he organized and was appointed captain of the Warren Rifles which later was assigned to the 19th Mississippi Regiment as Company C. During McClellan's Peninsula Campaign the following spring, Harris received commendations for his performance at Williamsburg where he was wounded; and as a result of his combat prowess during that engagement, Harris was promoted to major of the regiment. Following Sharpsburg the twenty-nine year old lawyer was promoted to lieutenant colonel and later assumed command of the 19th. Subsequently, Harris was promoted to colonel.[70]

A month after the battle, in his official report, Harris recalled his interpretation of Posey's order that fateful July afternoon:

> About 4 o'clock... I received orders to advance the right wing of my regiment until I encountered the enemy's skirmishers, and drive them back. I immediately deployed

the right wing on the brow of the hill in front of our batteries, and then advanced at a double quick about 250 paces [about 200 yards] through a wheat field to a post and rail fence [the western boundary of the Bliss Farm at the base of Seminary Ridge], where I came upon a line of skirmishers, and found the enemy occupying the [Bliss] orchard directly in my front. Lieutenant (C. W.) Burrage, Company A, of this regiment...who had been beyond the orchard and barn in the morning, informed me that, if I advanced with my skirmishers without my right being supported, there was imminent danger, from the nature of the ground, of my being flanked easily.

There Harris and his men waited until the 48th Mississippi moved into position on their right. Though Harris indicated that only about a half hour transpired until the 48th came up,[71] documentation suggests that the regiment did not arrive for at least another hour. Nonetheless, around 4:00 PM, as Harris' command had been stopped by the Federal skirmishers short of the Bliss Farmstead, Posey ordered the bulk of the 16th Mississippi forward to assist Harris.[72]

Among the Bliss Farm buildings, Captain Henry F. Chew, Company I, 12th New Jersey along with his acting first sergeant, George D. Bowen, were "seated in front of the house watching the [Confederates] as they threw shells and shot at [their] line."[73] Chew, a native of Claysville, Salem County, New Jersey:

gave early evidence of a desire for a military life, but the vigorous objections of his [Quaker] parents caused him to turn to the more peaceful occupation of a wheelwright at which he became very proficient.[74]

Nonetheless, in 1860 Henry joined the Johnson Guards at Salem and became their orderly sergeant, and after the firing on Fort Sumter, they were mustered into service as Company I, 4th New Jersey Volunteer Militia. Before the unit's term of enlistment expired at the end of July 1861, Chew had attained the rank of 1st lieutenant. Upon his return to his native state, he recruited men that were mustered into service as Company I, 9th New Jersey. This outfit later saw action during Burnside's Roanoke Expedition. However, due to a persistent fever, Henry could not complete his term of service and was forced to resign in early March 1862. Nevertheless, Chew recovered, recruited another company of men which became Company I, 12th New Jersey, and was commissioned its captain that August.[75]

28

At 5' 8" with green eyes and black hair, the twenty-five year old Chew was described as being a father figure:

> always with [them] in body and spirit... shared the hardships, joys and triumphs of the men.... Always gentle... never profane, never harsh, and never rash, always approachable, and thoughtful of the feelings of his boys; he commanded by love and respect, not by fear.[76]

Sergeant Bowen had a background similar to Chew. This nineteen year old native of Salem, New Jersey also had attended a Quaker School during his formative years, eventually graduating with high honors in 1857. At the outbreak of the war, George was an apprentice watchmaker and jeweler when he enlisted in the 12th New Jersey as a private. Though he had been promoted to fourth sergeant in September, 1862, Bowen had been made the acting 1st sergeant by the time of Gettysburg. He was described as "always ready, always reliable, and fruitful in the performance of every duty," and for his conduct during the battle, he was promoted to orderly sergeant on 4 July.[77]

As the Confederate shot and shell flew in the direction of the Bliss house, Sergeant Bowen suggested to Captain Chew "that [they] should move down to the barn where [they] would be out of the range of their guns." Chew replied that they were "as safe here as anywhere [.] You can't run away from them things," but according to Bowen, no sooner had the words left his captain's lips, that "a solid shot came and took the picket out of the fence [that Bowen] was leaning against... passing through the house [.]" Chew then decided to "get out of here,... [so, they] went down to the barn."[78]

As the shelling continued, at least Chew saw the proverbial handwriting on the wall. After the war, he recalled the situation. The Confederates had reinforced their skirmish line:

> This was not done at once, but a few men at a time so our attention would not be attracted until they had enough men to drive us away from the barn.[79]

Or so it appeared. Actually Chew was watching Posey's piecemeal deployment of the 48th, 19th, and 16th Mississippi Regiments, whose suspicious movements he reported "to the Lieutenant Colonel of the First Delaware [Edward Harris]" who was again in charge of Hays' skirmish line. When Chew advised him to report the situation to the officers on Cemetery Ridge and to request reinforcements, the "Lieutenant Colonel" replied "that he understood his business," that Chew was "under him, and that he [Harris] would take all the responsibility."[80] Shortly thereafter, the 16th Mississippi Regiment, commanded by Colonel Samuel E. Baker, advanced past the post and rail fence and the main Southern skirmish line.

Baker, a thirty-five year old former druggist from Natchez, entered the war during the spring of 1861 as captain of the Adams Light Guard #2, later designated Company D, 16th Mississippi. Described as "a good tactician, a first-rate disciplinarian and withal [retained] the love and respect of his entire command, [Baker was] marked as one of the best captains in his regiment." After the reorganization of the regiment in 1862, he "was elected major by a handsome majority." During the Seven Days Battles, at Cold Harbor, "Major Baker led his Regiment into the death full charge at the first assault on the enemy's works with such... coolness that the Regiment was loud in his praise." At Second Manassas again the observer "never saw an officer deport himself better." With the elevation of Posey to brigade command, Baker was promoted to colonel of the 16th Mississippi.[81]

As the sun sank low in the western sky, Colonel Baker and his men advanced into the Bliss orchard and chased the Union skirmishers back towards the farm buildings. As Sergeant Bowen later recalled:

> We were too few to stand them. [Looking] around [I] saw the men of the 1st Delaware, running to the rear [. As] my gun was loaded [I] decided I would not run with a loaded gun [. I] went into the garden of the house and tried to get a shot, [but] the yard or garden was filled with scrubbery [sic] so [I] could not see beyond. Seeing the men all running for the rear I [took] out after them, soon catching up with Lieut. Col. Harris of the 1st Del... [who] was getting to the rear as fast as he could.... [He] swung his sword around, called me a hard name, telling me to go back.... [This] I did not do but made a detour around him.[82]

After the retreat to the crest of Cemetery Ridge, Lieutenant Brady of the 1st Delaware witnessed a confrontation between Lieutenant Colonel Harris and General Hancock, the commander of the 2nd Corps. In Brian's orchard, Hancock:

> was standing erect in his stirrups interviewing him in the most choice and forcible language deemed suitable for the occasion which resulted in Harris being then and there, "ordered under arrest for cowardice in the face of the enemy."[83]

Nonetheless, the loss of the Bliss Farmstead did not go unnoticed. To the south, pickets of the 2nd Brigade, 2nd Division, 2nd Corps had watched the unfolding events with increased concern. The "Philadelphia Brigade" had been assigned a position on Cemetery Ridge to the left of Hays' Division in the vicinity of the Copse of Trees sometime after sunrise. At that time, Companies A and B of the 106th Pennsylvania were selected for picket duty, all under the command of Captain John J. Sperry (Company A) of the 106th.[84]

Upon reaching the Emmitsburg Road by the Nicholas Codori farm buildings, located about 600 yards south of the Bliss barn, Captain James C. Lynch and his Company B of the 106th were sent out on the advanced skirmish line. Initially, Lynch's detail advanced towards the northeast corner of Spangler's Woods, before the pickets of Scales, Posey and possibly Wright's commands forced them back. Returning to a more secure position, Lynch and the rest of the men of the Philadelphia Brigade's picket detachment watched along with Captain John L. Sparks and Company K of the 1st Delaware as the Bliss Farm buildings changed hands several times. The Philadelphia Brigade's skirmish line probably was the threatening force about which Colonel Harris of the 19th Mississippi had been warned by Lieutenant Burrage.[85]

However, with the advance of at least the 16th Mississippi shortly after 4:00 PM, Sparks' men had fallen back towards the crest of Cemetery Ridge with the rest of Hays' skirmish line which exposed the right flank of the Pennsylvanians to an enfilade coming from the Bliss buildings. Thus:

> Captain Lynch left his company... and went forward [from the picket reserve in the Emmitsburg Road] to ascertain the cause of the line giving way and finding the enemy in the possession of the house [barn] and pouring a flank fire upon our line of skirmishers [he] reported to Captain Sperry that the Bliss [barn] would have to be retaken or our line retire.[86]

Captain Sperry then ordered Lynch to retake the farm buildings, and thinking there was a small contingent of the Rebels occupying the premises, Lynch moved northward with only his company. The Confederates in the barn, "the whole 16th Mississippi..., allowed him to advance very close to them and demanded his surrender," which Lynch and his men refused to do. The Southerners then opened fire and drove Company B back to their picket reserve some 500 yards away. In this brief clash, the Pennsylvanians suffered twelve casualties, including one officer killed.[87]

31

During the last few days of August 1861, William H. Smith of Philadelphia enlisted in the 106th Pennsylvania and was appointed 1st Sergeant of Company B, followed fifteen months later by a promotion to 2nd Lieutenant. On 27 March 1863, after Smith had endured nearly eighteen months of arduous campaigning, he was granted leave, travelling from Falmouth, Virginia to reach Philadelphia by April Fool's Day, when he married Hannah Frances Little of Pennypack. But life was to play a cruel joke on the newlyweds, for Lieutenant Smith was killed in his company's charge on the Bliss barn. Eight months later, William H. Smith, Jr. was born three days after Christmas.[88]

The men of the 106th Pennsylvania were not the only ones attempting to hold their advanced positions. Northeast of the Bliss Farmstead, the four companies of the 4th Ohio were relieved about 4:00 PM by Lieutenant Colonel Carpenter, under orders from Carroll, and were replaced by Companies G and I of the 4th under the command of Captain Peter Grubb.[89]

Grubb must have been in pain as his picket detail advanced past the Emmitsburg Road, into the fields beyond, and towards the crest of the broad, flat knoll. During the Battle at Chancellorsville the previous May this twenty-six year old captain had received a debilitating wound to his left knee joint which involved some damage to his hamstring tendon.[90] Though he had recovered sufficiently to serve in the field, his old wound probably resulted in a painful limp.

Undoubtedly, as the Buckeyes advanced out onto the knoll, the 16th Mississippi had occupied the Bliss buildings and forwarded their skirmishers towards the Emmitsburg Road. The Buckeyes "soon drove the enemy before them, and took position to the left of an old frame house" (probably the Emanuel Trostle residence). According to Private Kepler, the Buckeyes "shielded themselves behind fence rails and ridges."[91]

Colonel Carroll, observing the effects of the Buckeye's deployment, realized that the Confederates would soon overrun Grubb's detachment. Some Graybacks already had reached the Emmitsburg Road only 170 yards west of the Brian barn. Thus, within minutes of Grubb's deployment, reinforcements were needed, and fast. Carroll then decided to send an entire regiment to the skirmish line, and he selected the 8th Ohio Volunteers, under Lieutenant Colonel Franklin Sawyer, for the mission.

Sawyer, only eleven days short of his thirty-eighth birthday, was a native of old Auburn, Ohio. He had attended Granville College and graduated from there with a law degree. Moving to Norwalk, Sawyer was appointed prosecuting attorney for Huron County and served as a militia officer. With the outbreak of hostilities, he enlisted in the 8th Ohio, initially for a three-month term of service, serving as captain of Company

D.[92] When the 8th Ohio was converted to a three-year regiment, Sawyer re-enlisted and joined his unit at Romney, West Virginia during November 1861, at which time he was promoted to lieutenant colonel. At 5' 11", large frame, dark complexion and deep-set eyes,[93] Sawyer was a prominent presence on the battle line.

Writing several years after the war, Sawyer eloquently described the advance of his regiment:

> The men loaded and capped their pieces and fixed bayonets, scaled the stone wall and formed. [I] jumped [my] horse over the wall, ordered the "double quick" which the regiment took up with a shout and dashed forward. The artillerymen of Robinson's [Hall's 2nd Maine] Battery and the batterymen at the Cemetery mounted their guns and waving their hats and flags, cheered us forward. The balls came thick and spitefully among us, the men began to fall, some killed, some wounded, but we swept [forward] until we came to the fence along the Emmitsburg Road.... The rebels fled... though some surrendered, but most of them hurriedly retreated down the slopes to their main line.[94]

But the men of the 8th Ohio did not stop at the Emmitsburg Road. They and possibly Grub's detachment swept the enemy before them. Up until the moment the Buckeyes reached the broad, flat knoll's crest, their movements were mostly hidden from the view of the Confederates in the vicinity of the Bliss house and along Stevens Run to the north. Though once Sawyer and his men crossed the crest they were in full view of the enemy, the Buckeyes continued to advance until they reached a Virginia or "worm" fence line on the knoll's military crest with their left flank resting only 270 yards from the Bliss house. There, Sawyer deployed Companies A and I as an advanced skirmish line under the command of Captain Anzor I. Nickerson before withdrawing the bulk of his men to the Emmitsburg Road near the Brian Tenant House. There he established regimental head-quarters in the roadbed opposite the dwelling. In this charge, Sawyer reported one man killed and thirteen wounded.[95] However, the Confederates still occupied the Bliss buildings.

As the Buckeyes advanced to the Emmitsburg Road, another assault was hastily organized to chase the pesky Rebel sharpshooters away from the Bliss buildings. The Confederate skirmishers had harassed the Union troops on Cemetery Ridge with their persistent small arms fire for almost an hour. About 4:30 PM, General Hays finally grew weary of this musketry and of the artillery shot and shell that landed about his positions. Near the Brian house, Captain A. Z. Stratton of the 12th New Jersey overheard a conversation between General Hays, Colonel Smyth, and Major John T. Hill, commander of the 12th. The topic was the Confederates posted in the Bliss barn:

> "Have you a regiment that will drive them out?," [asked Hays.]
> "Yes sir, the 12th will do it!," [answered Smyth. Then turning to Hill, he continued,] "but I don't want all of you, Major."[96]

The veteran 12th New Jersey Regiment was mustered into Federal service as Lee embarked on his Maryland Campaign in the fall of 1862. However, the Jerseymen would not "see the elephant" at Antietam. Instead, they were assigned to guard duty at Ellicott's Mill, Maryland until that December. On the 10th of that month, the regiment was ordered to Washington and then assigned to the 2nd Brigade, 3rd Division, 2nd Corps of Army of the Potomac. However, the 12th New Jersey would not reach the army near Fredericksburg until the 17th, four days after the Union blood bath on the plains before Marye's Heights. That winter the men endured the tedium of camp life and the futility of Burnside's "Mud March," and the following spring the regiment became entangled in Hooker's defeat at Chancellorsville.[97] At Gettysburg, the men of the 12th New Jersey were given another opportunity to show their mettle.

Their commanding officer, twenty-six year old Major Hill, was born in New Brunswick, New Jersey in July 1836. Before enlisting in the Union army, he had served as a bank clerk in New York City and as a captain of militia in his home town. After the outbreak of hostilities, Hill was appointed adjutant of the newly-formed 11th New Jersey Regiment and commenced recruitment activities. Enlistments were slow, but eventually a full complement was mustered into service and designated Company I. Hill first saw action at Fredericksburg in 1862 and the following April he was commissioned major and transferred to the 12th New Jersey. During Chancellorsville, after Colonel Willets was badly wounded and due to the incapacity of Lieutenant Colonel Davis, Hill took over command of the 12th.[98]

Upon returning to his regiment after his conference with Hays and Smyth, Hill assigned the job of driving the enemy troops out of the barn to Captain Samuel B. Jobes commanding the men of Companies B, E, G, and H. This detachment, numbering some 200 men, was pulled out of line, moved north past the Brian barn, and formed in columns by companies in a

34

"Yes sir, the 12th will do it!"

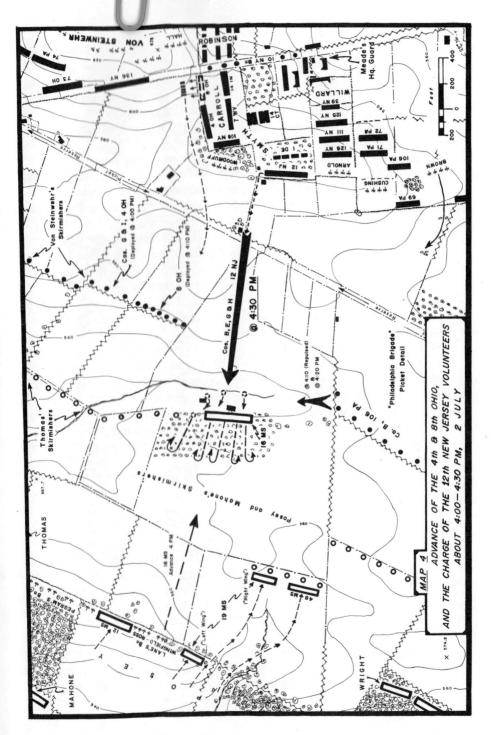

MAP 4

ADVANCE OF THE 4th & 8th OHIO,
AND THE CHARGE OF THE 12th NEW JERSEY VOLUNTEERS
ABOUT 4:00–4:30 PM, 2 JULY

35

small farm lane that linked the Brian farmstead with the Emmitsburg Road.[99] Immediately after the Buckeyes had swept the Confederates back towards Seminary Ridge, Colonel Smyth escorted the New Jerseyians to the picket reserve located along the Emmitsburg Road. As his aide, Captain Parsons, recalled it, the colonel led "them followed by his staff and orderlies... and [we] returned with bullets flying around us like drops of water in an April Shower."[100]

However, the detachment from the 12th New Jersey was not to be the only Federal troops to attack the barn. According to Lieutenant Brady, elements of the 1st Delaware also were to participate in the charge, and to the south, men from the 106th Pennsylvania prepared for a second assault to flush out the Southerners from the Bliss buildings.[101]

Thus, by happenstance around 4:30-5:00 PM, men of the 2nd Corps mounted a coordinated attack on both flanks of the Confederate forces in the Bliss buildings. The occupants of the barn – men from the 16th Mississippi, the 12th and 16th Virginia of Mahone's command,[102] and possibly others – did not notice the charge of the 12th New Jersey and elements of the 1st Delaware. Since the Confederates' attention was drawn towards the activities of the Buckeyes on the western slope of the broad, flat knoll to their left and towards the advancing Pennsylvanians to their right, they failed to see the Yankees move down to the Emmitsburg Road by the Brian Tenant House where they were screened from view by the knoll's crest. Moreover, the 12th New Jersey was armed with .69 caliber smoothbore muskets, whose ammunition was referred to as "buck and ball" – three lead buckshot packed with a lead musket ball. Thus as some 200 Jerseymen charged over the knoll towards the Bliss Farm yard, they packed weapons comparable to sixteen-gauge riot shotguns.

After the war, Sergeant Frank Riley of Company K, 12th New Jersey recalled the charge on the Bliss buildings:

> When we [Jobes' detachment] were within a short distance of the barn, our column halted, delivering their fire, then charged with a cheer, surrounding first the barn and then the house, the Rebels not surrendering until we poured in through the doors and windows and almost meeting them face to face, did [they] cry out for quarters: "We surrender Yanks – don't, don't shoot!"[103]

The attack was so enthusiastic that Colonel Smyth deemed it wise to send out one of his aides to insure that the Jersey troops did not advance too far. Smyth "directed" Captain Parsons to tell Captain Jobes not to advance

Farmstead. However, the latter two regiments never reached the Emmitsburg Road in force. Posey wrote in his official report that upon reaching the Bliss barn he found "[his] three regiments well up in advance." In reality he had witnessed the 48th Mississippi and the "right wing" of the 19th, attached to Wright's Brigade at or beyond the Emmitsburg Road, being supported by the left wing of the 19th. Colonel Harris' official report corroborated this scenario; he wrote:

> when General Wright's Brigade commenced advancing... I again gave the order to advance, pushing forward my line and driving the enemy from his position in the orchard, and capturing some prisoners at the barn. Still, driving the enemy before me, I advanced some 400 paces [about 300 yards] farther up the hill [Cemetery Ridge]. The left wing of my regiment, Major T. J. Hardin commanding, here came up to my support.[112]

At this critical moment, the Confederates were threatening to crack the Union center near the Copse of Trees. Why did not the 12th and 16th Mississippi regiments advance past the area of the Bliss buildings and Stevens Run to assist the 19th and 48th regiments attached to the left flank of Wright's Georgians?

By the late afternoon, the combat effectiveness of the 16th Mississippi Regiment was considerably reduced. Since mid-morning, detachments on picket duty had been under fire. Later, about 4:00 PM, the regiment advanced and cleared the Union skirmishers away from the Bliss buildings. Though supported by skirmishers from at least Mahone's command, when the Federals counterattacked, the 16th Mississippi, which had numbered some 385 men, suffered additional casualties, including many in the group of ninety-two who were captured at Bliss' barn.[113] To compound their exertions, both Sergeant James J. Kirkpatrick and an enlisted man in the 16th Mississippi indicated that the day was "hot" and that the men were "much exposed", suggesting the threat of sun stroke and heat prostration were ever-present dangers.[114]

Despite the arrival of Posey and some 370 men of the 12th Mississippi[115] to reinforce the 16th, the enfilade coming from the advanced skirmish line of Sawyer's and Grubb's Buckeyes posted to Posey's left front, behind the worm fence 270 yards away, prevented the Mississippians from advancing past the Bliss buildings and Stevens Run. Thus Posey, realizing that he needed additional troops to neutralize the Ohioans, requested Mahone to support his left with a regiment.

However, according to Posey, Mahone claimed he was under orders to move to the right, and could not comply. Contradictorily, Brigadier General Cadmus M. Wilcox (one of Anderson's brigadiers), in an addendum to his official report, and Wright, in a letter to his wife dated 7 July 1863, both maintained that Anderson had ordered not only Posey to advance, but Mahone as well, and that Anderson repeated the order.[116] But Mahone made no official mention of any requests coming from either Posey or his division commander to advance past the crest of Seminary Ridge. A week after the battle, Mahone simply wrote in his official report that:

> The brigade took no special or active part in the actions of that battle beyond that which fell to the lot [of] its line of skirmishers.
> During the days and nights of July 2 and 3, the brigade was posted in line of battle immediately in front of the enemy, and in support of Pegram's batteries. In this front, its skirmishers were quite constantly engaged, and, inflicted much loss upon the enemy.[117]

Thus the situation at the Bliss Farm around 6:45 PM stymied the Confederate en echelon attack. The skirmishers of the 4th and 8th Ohio, supported by those from Brigadier General Adolph von Steinwehr's Division of the 11th Corps, occupied a commanding position on the western slope of the broad, flat knoll. This Federal force, coupled with the lack of reinforcements being sent expeditiously to assist Posey, prevented Posey from adequately supporting Wright.

Nevertheless, as Posey was contemplating his situation at the Bliss Farm, and as Wright's Brigade with Posey's other two units were being repulsed near the Copse of Trees, another Confederate force prepared to advance. Thomas' and Perrin's Brigades of Pender's Division were aligned in battle formation on the crest of Seminary Ridge, in the vicinity of the McMillan buildings, about 600 yards northwest of the Bliss house. Shortly thereafter, in order to join up with the right flank of Brigadier General Stephen D. Ramseur's Brigade of Rodes' Division, Ewell's Corps, Thomas' and Perrin's men moved forward about 600 yards to a "sunken road" which was no more than a well-used farm lane. This lane extended out from town in a straight line towards the southwest, and after crossing Stevens Run, it made two ninety-degree turns, terminating at the northwest corner of the Bliss property. From this road Confederate officers probably debated the feasibility of a full-fledged frontal assault on Cemetery Hill, then brimming with Union artillery and further protected by the strong Yankee skirmish line posted along the crest of the broad, flat knoll to their immediate front.

About 7:00 PM, when Thomas' Brigade advanced to the Sunken Road to Posey's left rear, he had a problem similar to Posey's about half an hour earlier – the Buckeyes posted on the western slope of the broad, flat knoll. If Posey's troops and those of Pender's Division were to support Wright en echelon, Posey and/or Thomas needed to neutralize the threat of the Buckeyes to their front. That, in turn, would weaken Von Steinwehr's skirmish line with an enfilade from the south. With the knoll cleared of Federal troops, Posey could properly support Wright's advance. Moreover, Pender's infantry would have a protected marshalling area on the knoll's western slope from which to mount their main assault on Cemetery Hill, and artillery could be moved closer to blast the Federal positions at close range (about 600 yards).

However, Posey's regiments in the vicinity of the Bliss buildings could not or would not advance without support on their left to help eliminate the Buckeye threat, thereby preventing the Mississippians from assisting Wright's attack on the Union center. Consequently, with the repulse of Posey's right wing and Wright's Brigade, and due to the depleted condition of Posey's left wing, when Pender's Division was set in motion, his troops faced a stiff frontal fire from the Buckeyes and Von Steinwehr's men without adequate support on Thomas' right.

With the critical situation that had developed on the battle line along Stevens Run, another twist of fate directly affected the course of the fighting. By happenstance, the imaginary dividing line between divisional command spheres of A. P. Hill's Corps had been drawn just north of the Bliss house. When Pender's troops moved forward, Thomas' Brigade was stymied by the Union pickets on the broad, flat knoll. Theoretically, any appeal for Mahone to reinforce Thomas technically would have to have gone through Pender to A. P. Hill, and then through Anderson to Mahone. However, leadership from Hill was not forthcoming and most of the operations of the corps were left to the division commanders. Moreover, according to the official report of Pender's Division, earlier that afternoon Pender had gone "to the extreme right of his command, to advance his division should the opportunity offer."[118] William Dorsey Pender was one of the promising, rising stars in the Army of Northern Virginia, and during the war he had performed brilliantly in battle. However, as Pender was investigating the situation on his right, near the southeast corner of McMillan Woods, and in full view of the Bliss Farm and Sunken Road, an artillery shell burst nearby, inflicting what became a mortal wound. Subsequently, Pender was taken off the field and General Lane took command of the division.[119] This change in leadership had a destabilizing effect on the command structure and would further delay reaction time to the ever-changing situation on the battle lines. In the interim, Pender's

41

absence was felt. Apparently, no message was transmitted to Anderson requesting Mahone to support Thomas, for no such request was mentioned in the official reports of Anderson, Thomas or Mahone. Furthermore, even if a request had been forthcoming to Anderson, it probably was too late. With the repulse of his right three brigades (Wilcox, Perry and Wright), Anderson had even more impetus to retain Mahone's men on Seminary Ridge in case of a Union counterattack.

Therefore, a series of events caused the total breakdown of the Confederate en echelon attack: 1) A. P. Hill's non-involvement in combat operations; 2) the attention given by Anderson and Posey to the tactical situation at the Bliss Farm which resulted in the crucial deployment of the Ohio troops on the broad, flat knoll; 3) Mahone's inactivity; and 4) the untimely wounding of the highly competent Pender. Without reinforcements, Posey's left wing could not advance past the Bliss buildings to support the left flank of Wright's Brigade in its attack on the Union center around 6:30. Additionally, about thirty minutes later, still without reinforcements, Posey's troops were in no condition to support Thomas' Brigade in their attempts to move beyond the Sunken Road and Stevens Run to occupy the broad, flat knoll.

Consequently, the stalemate at the Bliss Farm remained unbroken. Posey's Mississippians and later Thomas' Georgians alone were to assault the Union skirmish line along the broad, flat knoll west of the Emmitsburg Road. Thus, fate provided the Buckeyes with the role of the proverbial thorn-in-the-side to the Confederate attacks.

During the late afternoon, Lieutenant Colonel Sawyer and Captain Grubb, with their respective commands, had been holding their own west of the Emmitsburg Road against the assaults of Posey and Thomas. After establishing their advanced position about 5:00 PM some 270 yards from the roadway, Sawyer withdrew the bulk of the 8th Ohio to the shelter of the Emmitsburg Road in the vicinity of the Brian Tenant House. The roadbed at that point formed a natural rifle pit, and as the soldiers reorganized, the dead and wounded were carried into the tenant house for protection.

Later, as Jobes' detachment of the 12th New Jersey withdrew from the Bliss Farmstead, some of the more adventurous Buckeyes "scrambled up into the garret of the old house, punched a hole through the roof and commenced firing upon the rebels." Sawyer wrote years later that:

> Their fire was instantly and fiercely answered which soon made our daring fellows "get out of that." Sergeant [William W.] Wells of Co. D was of the garret squad and hastened to inform me of the position of the rebels.[120]

Sawyer remembered that as the Confederates advanced towards the Buckeyes:

> Captain Nickerson was notified – but was already attacked
> by troops who had been concealed in a sunken road
> [elements of Posey and Thomas' commands] and also from
> concealed troops towards town [part of Thomas and
> Perrin's Brigade] and a sharp fire opened.... In a few
> minutes Nickerson was hotly engaged.[121]

As skirmishing increased in intensity, Sawyer ordered the rest of his 8th Ohio forward. The increased Yankee fire of the Buckeyes, bolstered with the musketry from the rest of the men of Von Steinwehr's skirmish line, was too much for the Confederate soldiers. The Southerners retreated back down the knoll, across Stevens Run, to the safety of the Sunken Road. Sawyer then reestablished his "pickets and lookouts" and withdrew the bulk of his regiment back to a line "several rods in front of [the Emmitsburg] road."[122]

Though the assaults were of great importance to the men on the skirmish line, the situation did not seem to cause a commotion back on the crest of Cemetery Ridge. Private Kepler of the 4th Ohio, stationed with the bulk of his regiment near Zeigler's Grove, stated simply that "Towards night several Confederate regiments... swept over our pickets... making increased havoc in the greatly thinned ranks, and taking several prisoners."[123]

Unbeknown to the Confederate officers as they reacted to the constantly changing situation along the battle lines around the Bliss Farm, the situation along the Union positions, in the vicinity of the Copse of Trees and Cemetery Hill, had deteriorated during the late afternoon and early evening hours.

General Hays had been sweating it out on Cemetery Ridge. About 5:00 PM, when the detachment of the 12th New Jersey charged the Bliss Farmstead, an urgent message was received from the Union left flank; the Confederates were destroying Sickle's 3rd Corps and reinforcements were desperately needed. About a half an hour later Colonel Willard's Brigade of New Yorkers was ordered to move by the left flank to a position about three-quarters of a mile to the south in order to assist in the repulse of the enemy north of the Abraham Trostle farmstead. The movement of Willard's Brigade depleted Hays' divisional strength by a third; only the men of Carroll's and Smyth's Brigades remained near Zeigler's Grove.

Concurrently, the Confederate artillery fire directed towards the area of Cemetery Hill grew more intense. Private Kepler of the 4th Ohio recalled that around 5:30 the Union artillery near the grove (Woodruff's and

Arnold's batteries) returned the enemy fire which, in turn, drew counter-battery fire from the Confederate line. As the Rebel shot and shell rained upon Zeigler's Grove, Kepler witnessed one round that shattered:

> a stack of guns of the rear regiment, the Seventh [West] Virginia, plunging a bayonet into a comrade's side and another cut a comrade of the 4th Ohio in twain; [and as the shelling continued,] there was hurrying to and fro, men for their companies and guns, disinterested eyewitnesses, generals and staff for shelter over the brow of the hill.... General Hays and his staff had just dismounted back of us, but across the brow of the hill, when a solid shot plowed through an orderly's horse. The batteries in front of us were now replying vigorously; the enemy skirmishers were making it hot for our pickets.[124]

Through this shot and shell, the Union artillerymen worked feverishly to respond to the Confederate challenge and to support the Federal pickets. According to 2nd Lieutenant John Egan of Woodruff's battery:

> About 6 o'clock, when the heavy fighting was going on on the extreme left of our line of battle, in addition to a heavy artillery [fire], a line moved up in front of the battery [Posey's left wing and Thomas's command] and a sharp fight occurred. Canister was used during the whole of this time to dislodge and keep down this line, as it succeeded in getting good cover behind a ditch [either the Emmitsburg Road or Stevens Run].[125]

The enemy must have been fairly close to Woodruff's battery position if the Yankees used "canister" the whole time as Egan claimed. The average effective range of Civil War canister was about 400 yards. Apparently Egan's memory was cloudy, for his cannoneers probably did not fire that large-sized buckshot into the backs of the Yankee skirmishers. The Buckeyes left no accounts indicating they were hit by friendly fire. Moreover, the area of the Bliss Farm buildings and Stevens Run were beyond the effective range of canister. Possibly Egan's section (two guns) was firing canister towards the southwest and at the left flank of Posey's right wing attached to Wright's Brigade as those Confederates threatened the Union center. Meanwhile the rest of Woodruff's batterymen may have bombarded the enemy to the west with a type of "long-range canister" called case shot.

Whatever the situation was, a short distance to the south, the rest of Hazard's 2nd Corps artillery was very busy plastering the Mississippians and Georgians with canister at close range. An artilleryman in Arnold's battery wrote in his diary that:

> Our battery was in action all afternoon... [raging] until nine o'clock in the night. One time it seemed as if we were all surrounded. Battery A, Fourth regulars [Cushing's] reversed their pieces ready to fire to the rear.[126]

As part of Lee's strategy for the second day, General Ewell's troops attacked the Federal right at Spangler's Spring and Culp's Hill, but these attacks were not coordinated with Longstreet's assaults on the Yankee left. Three hours passed before Southern infantry entered the fray on Culp's Hill, and that delay gave Meade the opportunity to strip troops from that sector and better utilize them to repulse Longstreet's attack.

The Confederate high command had no way of knowing that the Union right was so vulnerable. By dusk (about 8:30), after an hour of fighting, the Southerners had maneuvered past the abandoned Union rifle pits near Spangler's Spring, halting only 500 yards from the unprotected rear of the Union army. Southern forces also had managed to rout the remnants of the Union 11th Corps on the eastern summit of Cemetery Hill, capturing several artillery pieces in the process. These events were taking place about 1,000 yards away from Cushing's position. About 7:00-8:30 PM the artillery pieces probably were reversed to cover any possible enemy breakthrough on East Cemetery Hill. Subsequently Hays was ordered to send the bulk of Carroll's Brigade to bolster the Yankee infantry there, and, again, Hays' effective strength was reduced. Only Grubb's two companies of the 4th Ohio, Sawyer's 8th Ohio, and Smyth's Brigade were left to hold the Zeigler's Grove sector. However, about one-third of Hays' remaining units had been engaged during the day's skirmishing about the Bliss Farm.

Thus, the time from 6:30-8:30 PM was one of the most critical periods of the Battle of Gettysburg. Posey and Thomas attacked and were stymied by the Buckeyes and Von Steinwehr's pickets west of Zeigler's Grove. Perrin's and Ramseur's skirmishers probed the Union picket line around the northwestern base of Cemetery Hill and threatened a full-scale attack. Concurrently, Ewell's troops assaulted East Cemetery Hill. Meanwhile, in the Zeigler's Grove-Cemetery Hill sector of the Union line, Hays' Division was stripped down to one-third of its effective strength when Williard was sent to assist Sickles and the bulk of Carroll's Brigade was sent to support the Yankees on East Cemetery Hill. The only reserve troops left in the area that were close enough to respond to an emergency at a moment's notice

45

was Robinson's Division of the 1st Corps which was posted on the southern slopes of Cemetery Hill. However, the combat effectiveness of these demoralized troops was questionable, for during the previous day's fighting Robinson's numerical strength had been reduced to 900 men. Although the Union 6th Corps had arrived on the field, it would take time for orders to be dispatched; then those troops would have to be put in motion and marched as far as a mile at the double-quick to reach the Cemetery Hill sector, all after their grueling thirty-five mile forced march from the Manchester, Maryland area. The only troops on Cemetery Hill that had not been heavily engaged were those of Colonel Orlando Smith's 2nd Brigade of Von Steinwehr's Division, numbering about 1,600 effectives; Smith's pickets had been supporting the right of the Buckeye skirmishers.[127]

However, the Bliss Farm struggle stopped the en echelon mode of attacks by halting the brigades of Thomas, Perrin, and Ramseur's along the Sunken Road. Thus, only Ewell's troops assaulted Cemetery Hill, and neither the effectiveness of Robinson's and Von Steinwehr's troops nor the alacrity of the 6th Corps were tested. As a result, the bulk of Carroll's Brigade was sufficient to roust Ewell's Confederates from East Cemetery Hill.

Colonel Harris of the 19th Mississippi reported the activities of the right wing of Posey's Brigade between the hours of 6:30 PM and dusk. While their fellow Mississippians were stymied at the Bliss buildings, the right wing had accompanied Wright's Brigade in their assault on the Union center, moving east of the Emmitsburg Road:

> Still driving the enemy before me.... Within 60 yards of the right of my line of skirmishers was a battery of the enemy [Battery B, 1st Rhode Island Light Artillery] which was playing upon General Wright. My skirmishers succeeded in driving the gunners three different times from their guns, when they changed their position to the crest of the hill.[128]

As Wright's Georgians and Posey's Mississippians advanced, forcing the right flank of Sickles' 3rd Corps to fall back to Cemetery Ridge, Lieutenant T. Fred Brown's Battery B had been rolled forward to an outcropping of rocks several yards in front of the Union line near the Copse of Trees. There the artillerymen assisted in covering the retreat of the Union infantry. As Wright's Brigade swept past the Codori farmstead, the Union cannoneers, firing canister, received a severe fire from the Confederate skirmishers. In this assault the Southern troops were able to temporarily capture Brown's guns. However, due to the retreat of supporting troops on Wright's right flank, the artillery fire coming from Cushing's, Arnold's, and part of Woodruff's batteries, and several infantry charges that were made on both flanks, by the 15th Massachusetts and part of the Philadelphia Brigade, Wright's Georgians and the supporting Mississippians withdrew to the area west of the Emmitsburg Road. Nearly 200 Southern stragglers left in the Codori's orchard were captured.[129]

Near the Bliss buildings around dusk, General Posey, who had witnessed the assaults of his brigade and those of Wright and Thomas, sent Anderson a message informing him of the disposition of his troops. A short time later, Posey was ordered to withdraw to his original position supporting Pegram's Battalion of artillery on Seminary Ridge, leaving a detachment on the skirmish line.[130] According to a Confederate in the 16th Mississippi, "Co. C lost 4 men captured and 4 wounded, including Captain Shay."[131]

At about 9:00 PM, Willard's battle-weary brigade returned to Cemetery Ridge. Colonel Eliakim Sherrill of the 126th New York, who assumed command after Willard was killed, returned the brigade to Zeigler's Grove and halted it in the rear of Arnold's battery. The brigade had suffered heavy casualties in the defense of the main Union line after Sickles' troops had withdrawn from the Emmitsburg Road. According to official reports, 714 men out of approximately 1,500 engaged during the three days of battle, were casualties. Many of these were inflicted on 2 July.[132]

About 11:00 PM the men of Captain Grubb's detachment of the 4th Ohio were relieved of picket duty and returned to their regiment which was then located on the East Cemetery Hill. According to Private Kepler, Companies G and I:

> probably sustained greater loss in proportion than any two companies of any one regiment in the entire army; Company G had eight killed during three years and three months [of war,] six of those fell during the storm of shot and shell and the charge on this fatal afternoon.... [Of this detachment, half] had been killed or wounded... [and five were listed as missing].[133]

Captain Grubb was among the wounded. A musket ball had split the radial bone of his left forearm in half and forced him to leave the field after placing his detachment under the guidance of Sergeant Martin V. B. Longsworth. Though Longsworth, too, had been wounded, he was a determined soldier who refused to quit the field without direct orders from his superiors. As the remnants of this intrepid band made their way towards

East Cemetery Hill, members of the "Pioneer Corps" brought off their wounded, buried their dead, and marked the graves.[134]

Among the dying was 2nd Lieutenant Addison H. Edgar, whose complexion, hair and eyes were described as being black – like the coal that was used to fuel the iron furnaces in his native Allegheny County, Pennsylvania. This 5' 7 1/2" tall Ohioian had attained the age of twenty-three years at the time of his demise at Gettysburg. Mustered into service for three years on 6 June 1861, Addison was immediately appointed 2nd Sergeant of Company G, and by January 1862 he was promoted to 1st Sergeant. Edgar endured the trials and hardships of his regiment and was promoted to 2nd Lieutenant on 29 March 1863. However, Edgar's luck was ebbing. At Chancellorsville on 3 May, he was seriously wounded in the shoulder which resulted in a stint in a general hospital in Washington. But he recuperated in time to rejoin his unit which was then attempting to overtake Lee's Pennsylvania-bound army. Lieutenant Edgar was issued a pass that allowed him to rejoin the 4th Ohio, and Addison caught up with his unit on or about 22 June. Under the orders of Lieutenant Colonel Carpenter, he was assigned to Company G.[135] Ten days later, Edgar and 2nd Lieutenant Samuel J. Shaub were listed among the dying or dead. As Edgar drew his last few breaths, he summed up the contribution of the Buckeyes that day – he requested that his comrades return his watch and sword to his parents and to assure them that he had been "true to their trust."[136]

During the heated skirmishing on the Bliss Farm that day, the last three fresh regiments of Smyth's Brigade had been deployed where General Hays thought they would do the most good.

The 10th New York Battalion numbering about 100 men – a mere shell of the old 10th New York Regiment – had been deployed in rear of the 3rd Division as a provost guard. According to Lieutenant William P. Seville, acting assistant adjutant to Colonel Smyth, the battalion was positioned on the reverse slope of Cemetery Ridge along the Taneytown Road. "There they were posted as skirmishers about ten paces between men." Apparently General Hays wanted to insure that no one would tarnish the reputation of his command by fleeing the front lines at a critical moment, for Major George F. Hopper, commander of the battalion, stated in his official report that he was ordered "to deploy in rear of the Third Division, for the purpose of arresting stragglers."[137]

The second regiment, the 108th New York initially arrived on the field shortly after daybreak and deployed in rear of the 10th New York Battalion on the reverse slope of the ridge. About 8:00 AM, the 108th was moved to the right and was positioned in Zeigler's Grove as a support for Woodruff's battery. There, the regiment remained for the rest of the day and suffered some casualties during the artillery exchanges, but it was not actively engaged.[138]

Lastly, the 14th Connecticut Volunteers were not deployed on the front line until approximately 5:00 PM, when Captain Jobes' detachment of the 12th New Jersey charged the Bliss buildings. The 14th had been assigned to picket duties the previous evening (1 July). Around 7:00 AM the regiment was relieved and marched up the Taneytown Road towards Meade's headquarters, arriving there an hour later. According to Chaplain Henry S. Stevens, the men then crossed the road "at a low point" and marched across the fields south of the Leister House, then turning right (north), they filed past the barn "into the field beyond the barn lane." This placed the 14th east of the Brian House and Zeigler's Grove and on the reverse slope of Cemetery Ridge.[139]

The 14th Connecticut was mustered into service on 23 August 1862 near New Haven and was placed under the command of Colonel Dwight Morris. The troops were described as "young men of good character [with] no less than eighty-six towns... represented" by the 1,015 recruits. Their journey to the seat of war brought them to central Pennsylvania, having been shipped to Harrisburg after nearly being sent to Chambersburg. However, the regiment was diverted to Baltimore where the 14th passed in review for General Wool, who commented to Morris, "A splendid regiment, not one drunk man in the ranks, too good of a regiment to be sent anywhere but to the front!" Consequently, the 14th was sent to Camp Chase in the defenses around Washington, and on 7 September, the New Englanders were brigaded with two other regiments, including the 108th New York. Colonel Morris was placed in overall command. Ten days later, men of Morris's Brigade of the 2nd Corps had their baptism of fire in front of the infamous Bloody Lane at Antietam.[140]

During the nine months between the battles at Antietam and Gettysburg, the 14th Connecticut's effective strength was considerably reduced. After Antietam, unsanitary conditions and the inability of the surgeons "to cope with the various diseases and ailments... [reduced the] muster roll day by day," and as the regiment reached Falmouth opposite Fredericksburg, the 14th could muster only eight officers and 200 enlisted men. By July, 1863 only 160 men were fit for duty.[141]

One of the most eloquent writers of the 14th Connecticut was the Reverend Henry Smith Stevens. Born in Middletown, Middlesex County, Connecticut on 14 October 1832 to David and Nancy A. (Smith) Stevens, Henry had heeded some inner calling for the ministry early in his life. Nonetheless, tragedy struck during the summer of 1858 as if God was testing his faith as He had done with Job. Stevens' wife, Mariella, had taken sick and died of consumption on that 11 July at the age of twenty-seven years and six months. Although he remarried, by the late spring of 1862, Stevens decided to leave his second wife, Eliza, and his pulpit in Cromwell, situated near the banks of the Connecticut River, in order to accept the position as the chaplain of the 14th.[142]

The men of his regiment loved to tease and play practical jokes on Reverend Henry. One soldier recounted the time when the chaplain had fallen asleep writing. A lieutenant came along and placed an empty liquor bottle under his arm. Until Stevens awoke, the sight of a chaplain apparently in a drunken stupor was the source of countless chuckles.[143]

As the men of the 14th Connecticut awaited orders, some of the men, including Stevens, walked up to the crest of Cemetery Ridge, and watched the skirmishing that was in progress on the Bliss Farm. Twenty-eight years later Stevens described what he saw:

> The scene on the broad glacis between the hostile lines on that fine summer morning was charming and the work of the sharpshooters as we watched it grew almost fascinating, we forgetting, nearly, that the game was human. One marksman had made his quarry a wounded skirmisher (one half mile away) unable to stand, who was trying, by a series of flops, to drag his body up the slope to the shelter of his own lines. The marksman fired at him for several minutes as frequently as he could load and take aim; but we confess to a feeling of relief and gladness, ...when the [sharpshooter] let up on the poor fellow... [failing] to hit him. Truly, war makes game of men, and we all [do act] reckless in our treatment of human life.

Stevens also noticed that the ambulances were "venturing out far in front to pick up our wounded skirmishers."[144]

Evidently, the 1st Company of Andrews' Sharpshooters had their specialty perfected. An officer in the 12th New Jersey described Stevens' scene with a different eye, but made a similar comment on the morality of that type of warfare. The men were armed with "very long-range telescopic rifles, with a sort of tripod rest. [They] were placed on our main line with instructions to stop [the] annoyance" of their Confederate counterparts in and around the Bliss barn. After a time the Southern sharpshooters became wise to the range of the rifles and the accuracy of the Massachusetts marksmen. "Several men were seen to fall at the openings in the barn, [but the Confederate sharpshooters]... became more and more cautious." They realized that at the flash of a rifle discharging along Cemetery Ridge, they should duck out of view. When the ball passed through the opening, they would" instantly reappear, ready to try a shot or fall back again if a second rifle flashed on our line." Andrews' Sharpshooters, though, were quick learners:

> To meet these new tactics,... they formed themselves into squads or partnerships of three, and when the three were ready with correct aim, number one would fire; the enemy would instantly retire from the two openings; then counting "one, two, three," the remaining partners would fire simultaneously, each at his appointed opening; the ball from number one passing through the opening, the enemy immediately reappeared, too late to see the flash of the second rifles, yet in time to receive their bullets. Alas! how little we thought human life was the sake for which this game was being played.[145]

About noon, as Hays was attempting to stabilize his skirmish line for a second time that day, the 14th Connecticut was moved up the slope of Cemetery Ridge to assist the men of the 108th New York Regiment who were supporting Woodruff's battery. Sometime later during one of the exchanges of artillery fire, the regiment suffered its first casualty of the battle; a rather embarrassing and humorous one. Apparently as the boom of the Union artillery intermixed with the explosions of Confederate shells, the horse of a staff officer became rather fidgety. The officer, instead of walking the horse off to the rear or enlisting the aid of a nearby infantryman, selected a drummer boy for the task. After the youth mounted, a shell apparently burst nearby, for the horse bolted towards the rear carrying the poor, helpless boy and his drum along for the ride. As the panic-stricken animal skedaddled, it headed straight for the men of the 14th Connecticut. Luckily, most of the soldiers moved out of the way, except Captain James B. Coit, Company K. As he rose drawing his sword, the captain was knocked senseless when he was hit squarely in the face by the breast of the beast. This caused Coit's face to swell, "totally closing his eyes for a time." Chaplain Stevens then escorted the injured officer to a field hospital (probably the one at the Catherine Guinn Farm along the Taneytown Road).[146]

Several hours later, between 4:00 and 5:00 PM, the 14th Connecticut was ordered to move to the left and deployed in a single line behind the 1st Delaware which supported Arnold's battery to their left and the 12th New Jersey to their right. About dusk, Companies A and F were deployed as skirmishers along the Emmitsburg Road to Hays' front.[147] The Confederates, however, were able to retain possession of the Bliss Farmstead and had established their own picket line.

Though the night passed in relative quietness, it did not pass without several incidents. Along the advanced skirmish line of the 8th Ohio, at least two Confederates were observed foraging for food. Second Lieutenant Thomas H. Thornburg informed Lieutenant Colonel Sawyer many years after the battle that his men:

> downed a rebel soldier that evening who was actually fighting with four fair-sized hams strung over his shoulders, and another with a cheese "as big as a grindstone" [probably purloined from the Bliss kitchen and smokehouse].[148]

Later, about midnight, the Confederates "opened a hot fire" according to 1st Lieutenant Thomas F. Galway of the 8th Ohio. During the last minutes of 2 July, someone was heard approaching the Union skirmish line:

> At first I thought it was a deserter, but the clanking of his sword showed that he was an orderly with instructions for someone.... "Where is General Ramseur's Brigade?" [asked the figure]. Sergeant [John G.] Fairchild, who lay along side of me, replied, "There" thinking to decoy him, but Private Brown who [was] generally called "Bucktown," not being so polite cocked his gun. The click of the hammer alarmed our bird and he turned and fled. [As Galway described it, the incident] caused a lively fire for a few moments.[149]

Possibly, the lost Confederate was Acting Sergeant Blackwood Benson of the 1st South Carolina Regiment. Born and raised in the town of Hamburg, South Carolina, Blackwood was barely sixteen years old when he and his brother Berry were mustered into service at Charleston during the early summer of 1861.[150]

On 7 July 1863, Blackwood wrote of his experiences during the battle near Gettysburg. "Shortly after dusk" of 2 July, he recalled that his unit received orders to support the advance of Ramseur's Brigade, but the orders were later countermanded. These events "left pickets in advance of ours, and Lt. Sharp was ordered to join the left of his pickets with the right of Ramseur's." When this intrepid band of South Carolina sharpshooters could not locate the right of Ramseur's skirmish line at the designated place, Benson was ordered by Sharp to reconnoiter and ascertain where

Ramseur's right was situated. With the moon lighting a cloud-covered sky, Benson located a fence nearby and began to follow it towards the Union lines. After walking about fifty yards, he halted when he saw a line of unidentified skirmishers straddling the same fence line some seventy-five yards to his front. Being too dark to discern whose pickets they were, Benson "got on his belly and <u>snaked</u> it about 25 yards farther" where he noticed that the unidentified skirmishers' uniforms were dark in color. Guessing that they were Yankees, Benson reported this information to Sharp, but the lieutenant informed him that he had to confirm the identity of the skirmishers:

> I went back very cautiously and got about 50 yards from them (as well as I can remember) and the following occurred:
> Benson: (in a loud voice) "Whose pickets are those."
> Reply: "Our pickets."   The "our" <u>sounded</u> Confederate. [A pause of about a minute ensued.]
> Benson: "To which side do you belong?"
> Reply: "Whose side do you belong?"
> Benson: "The Rebels."
> Reply: "Well, we are for the Union."

According to Blackwood, he "dried up for five minutes and then shouted, "Are these pickets from General Ramseur's Brigade?" Private Benson was answered by a few shots from the shadowy forms to his front. A short time later, he repeated the question, but this time a voice answered him very close by. Believing that he was about to be captured, Benson decided to crawl back to his company which, in the interim, "had fallen back a little."[151]

To the south, some of the skirmishers of the 14th Connecticut found themselves in a real pickle. After Company A had deployed near the Emmitsburg Road, four men – Sergeants Henry M. Cody and John Geatly, Corporal William Jacobs, and Private James W. French – were ordered to move from the picket reserve in the roadway to the advance skirmish line. As these intrepid soldiers advanced towards the Bliss buildings in the moonlit darkness, several "Johnnies" jumped up and captured them. When they were interrogated by the Confederate officer in charge, Corporal Jacobs:

> who... had something of a way with words and a mighty storyteller, took great pains to enlighten his custodians with amplified accounts of the immense hosts of

Pennsylvania militia that were coming... as reinforcements.[152]

Corporal Jacobs could not know at the time that his story was not that far from the truth.

Apparently the New Englanders were not the only ones captured on picket duty that evening, for a member of the 16th Mississippi recorded:

> One light note: Last night [2-3 July] Col. W. H. Taylor's men [12th regiment] captured 60 pickets without firing a shot. How is this done? If men are trapped, with muskets trained on them, it ['s] either surrender or die....[153]

As the skies east of Gettysburg began to brighten, promising a third, muggy day of fighting, Companies B and D of the 14th Connecticut replaced A and F on picket duty.[154]

Chapter Four

3 JULY 1863
"NO LIBBY FOR US."
"... ONE FOURTEENTH MAN WAS
EQUAL TO ANY TWO."

With the arrival of the last few remaining units of his army, Lee made some hard decisions that would affect the course of American History. Despite his setbacks, Lee began to prepare for the continuation of his strategy of 2 July. In his official report, Lee wrote:

> The result of this [second] day's operations induced the belief that, with proper concert of action, and with the increased support that the positions gained on the right [Little Round Top area] would enable the artillery to render the assaulting columns, we should ultimately succeed, and it was accordingly determined to continue the attack. The general plan was unchanged. Longstreet, re-enforced by Pickett's three brigades, ... was ordered to attack the next morning, and General Ewell was directed to assail the enemy's right at the same time. [Emphasis added.][155]

During the late evening hours of 2 July, Ewell's troops had been reinforced in preparation for their renewed assault on the Union right. However, the following morning, the Yankees stole the initiative. At 4:00 AM, the Federal attack began a struggle for Spangler's Spring and Culp's Hill that continued for seven consecutive hours. Moreover, Longstreet, still nursing his grand flanking movement stratagem which Lee had refused to incorporate into his general plan the previous day, either misread, modified, or interpreted Lee's instructions too liberally. When Lee went to see him that morning and realized that Longstreet's troops were not ready to coordinate with Ewell, Lee realized that his plan had to be scrapped.[156] After Lee, Longstreet, and several staff officers had made another reconnaissance of the Union positions that morning, an alternative plan of attack evolved. An assault was to be made on the Union center – Lee's last chance to defeat Meade's army. However, the Bliss Farm quagmire again affected the Confederate stratagem.

As the sun began to light the Friday morning sky, promising another hot, humid day, the serenity was shattered by the sounds of the Union attacks on Ewell's troops. With the Union artillery firing on the Confederate positions near Culp's Hill, the all too brief rest of Hays' troops ended. "The early morning firing... disturbed somewhat our slumbers on the ridge, but not enough to wake us thoroughly," wrote Chaplain Stevens.[157] Nonetheless, sparring about the Bliss Farmstead was about to be renewed.

By the morning of 3 July, the command structure of the 1st Delaware was in disarray. With the arrest of Lieutenant Colonel Harris the previous afternoon, control of the unit devolved on the senior company commander, Captain Thomas B. Hizar, (Company I). Hizar, though wounded, retained command until 11:00 PM when, according to the regiment's official report, Lieutenant William Smith (Company A) was placed in charge.[158]

Nonetheless, about twenty-three years after the battle, Lieutenant Brady stated in his letter to Bachelder that he was the senior 1st lieutenant of the 1st Delaware, and that it was he who commanded the regiment until Harris returned on 7 July. Brady commented that he never filed an official report because he was too busy with the fine art of running a regiment. However, Lieutenant John Dent did find the time to submit a regimental report on Gettysburg.[159]

Whatever the situation was, early that morning Brady claimed to have received an order from General Hays "to take and hold the barn at all hazards."[160] Around 7:00 AM, Brady returned to the regiment and called for volunteers, and the resulting detachment consisted of twenty-seven men of the 1st Delaware and four or five men from the 12th New Jersey. When assembled, Brady's little band moved along the ridge to the area immediately north of the Brian barn and after "divesting [themselves] of all superfluous articles such as haversacks, sword, scabbards, & c.," they charged towards the Bliss barn. However, the Confederate skirmishers proved too much for this small detachment, for after the Federals advanced "to within fifty feet of the barn, ... [they] were checked by a withering fire from the various vents... and compelled to retire." Of this small band, nearly all were casualties; two were killed (Corporal John B. Sheets and Private William J.

Dorsey, both of Company D, 1st Delaware) and approximately twenty-four wounded.[161]

Nearby the men of Woodruff's, Arnold's, and Cushing's batteries began to return the intermittent fire of the Confederate artillery and of the sharpshooters in the Bliss barn who had fired upon Brady's little band. According to Sergeant Frederick Fuger of Cushing's battery, the men were:

> annoyed by sharpshooters firing from a barn (Bliss...), hence Battery "A" opened with case shot and shell and within a few minutes the barn was evacuated by the Confederate sharpshooters.[162]

This drew counter-battery fire from the Confederates who shelled the Federals in the vicinity of the Brian Farm, but the Yankee artillery did not respond in kind until about 8:00 AM. Fuger wrote that Cushing and Major General Henry J. Hunt, Meade's chief of artillery:

> were standing in rear of No. 3 limber... [when] an explosion took place, three limbers #1, 2, and 3, exploding.... The first limber was struck, which caused the... [others] to explode.... [No one was injured, but] little reply was made.[163]

As Lieutenant Egan recalled years later, "batteries opened at intervals from different points along the whole Rebel line upon the artillery of the 2nd Corps," and there were at least "ten or twelve distinct artillery fights" that morning.[164] The occasional incoming rounds were bothersome, and to compound the annoyance, the "returning [enemy] occupants [of the Bliss barn] soon sent the little stingers [bullets] flying around us as before."[165]

At 5' 7", weighing approximately 150 pounds and with light hair and blue eyes, William A. Arnold did not cut a dashing appearance on Cemetery Ridge that morning. Born on 4 September 1830 at Cranston, Rhode Island, Arnold, a former bookkeeper in Providence, had enlisted in the early fall of 1861. Assigned to Randolph's Battery E, 1st Rhode Island Light Artillery, Arnold was sent to Fort Monroe and remained there for fifteen months. In April 1862 while on duty on the Virginia Peninsula, Arnold was involved in an accident that nearly ended his military career. The horse on which he was riding fell on top of him, injuring his spine and causing paralysis on his right side and leg. He recovered and was involved in the closing phases of the Seven Days Battles where he was wounded in his sore right leg at Malvern Hill. After recovering from his wound, though plagued by chronic pain, Arnold was promoted to commander of Battery A.[166]

During 2 July, Arnold and his cannoneers endured the harassment of the sharpshooters' fire which emanated from the Bliss Farm. By the morning hour of the Third, he was irritated and complained to Colonel Smyth and General Hays. A short time later, Hays ordered the barn to be retaken.[167] For this mission, men of the 12th New Jersey were selected once more. Receiving orders from Hays via Colonel Smyth, Major Hill selected companies A, C, D, F, and K for this rather hazardous duty and placed Captain Richard S. Thompson of Company K in command.[168]

Richard Swain Thompson was born in Cape May Court House, New Jersey two days after Christmas 1837. At the age of thirteen, he entered Norristown Academy near Philadelphia and continued on to graduate from Harvard law school in 1861. The following year, Thompson was admitted to the bar at Philadelphia, and during his residency there, he joined Captain Biddle's Artillery Company. In August 1862, within a ten-day period, Thompson enlisted a full company of men from Cumberland County, New Jersey. The group was mustered into service as Company K of the 12th New Jersey Regiment with Thompson as its captain. Later, during his regiment's stay at Ellicott's Mill, Maryland, the twenty-five year old Thompson was appointed assistant provost-marshall under General Wool, undoubtedly due to his prestigious legal education. In February 1863, he was appointed as a judge-advocate on a divisional court-martial board.[169]

Similar to Arnold, the men of the 12th New Jersey had endured the harassment of the Confederate sharpshooters, but now Thompson and his detachment had a chance to chase the "Johnnies" out of the Bliss barn. Accompanying the New Jerseyians as support were Lieutenant Brady and "that part of the First Delaware... not on the skirmish line." In all, the detachment numbered about 200 men.[170] About 8:00 AM, Captain Thompson led his men up to the Brian barn, down the farm lane, and across the Emmitsburg Road to a point a short distance to the west. There the Jerseymen formed into columns by companies, using the crest of the broad, flat knoll as partial cover. As soon as they were in formation, with Company F in the van, the detachment charged the barn.[171]

When the men cleared the crest, they were "exposed to the concentrated fire of the whole Rebel picket line."[172] According to Captain Thompson:

> As soon as the distance would justify, the five companies brought their muskets to trial arms and charged at double quick. They carried the [enemy] skirmish line and rushed onward for the barn, but before they could reach it the enemy's [picket] reserve... broke from their protection, and

scattering over the field [they] ran to cover in a thick
growth of low bushes to the rear and north of the barn.[173]

Not only were the Federals in plain view of the Confederates around the
Bliss buildings, but they were probably surprised to see in the Sunken Road
near the Stevens Run, Thomas's troops who had been screened from their
view by the knoll. As the Jerseymen charged towards the barn in their
compact formation, the Confederates began to enfilade the Yankee column.
In the charge, Privates William H. H. Stratton, George W. Adams, William
H. Johnson, James R. Russell, and 1st Lieutenant John J. Trimble – all of
Company F – were hit by enemy fire.[174]

As they reached the barn, the Federals ran under the forebay and
entered the stable area. Some men climbed to the main floor as the last few
Confederates skedaddled out of the rear of the building, fleeing into the
Bliss orchard. When Sergeant James White entered the stable, he ran to a
basement window on the opposite side hoping to take a few parting shots at
the retreating "Johnnies." As he aimed his rifle out of the opening, a
Confederate who was backed up against the wall next to the window but on
the outside, and whom the sergeant had not seen until he raised his arms,
yelled, "Don't shoot I'll give up," probably startling the Union soldier. After
the war, White wrote that the Southerner "accepted the invitation to come
in through the window without hesitation."[175]

A short time later, Corporal Abel K. Shute moved into the open
doorway on the main floor. Shute, a twenty-two year old farm boy from
Mullica Hill, Gloucester County, New Jersey had taken part in the
preliminary meetings that resulted in the formation of Company F. He had
been described by a fellow soldier as possessing:

> fine personal appearance and [was] correct in his habits,
> with a strong religious feeling, that often led him to check
> the wild exuberance of some of his comrades.... [He had
> been appointed corporal because of] performing his duties
> with conscientious care.[176]

As Shute scooted across the open doorway, a Confederate marksman
in the Bliss orchard shot him in both knees, and while sprawled on the barn
floor, he started "calling loudly for help." Sergeant White turned over his
prisoner to Sergeant H. M. Avis, and then went to the corporal's assistance.
Shute lingered for four weeks before he died at a hospital in Baltimore.[177]

At the time of the 12th New Jersey's assault, only a few Confederates
occupied the barn, probably due to Cushing's shelling a short time earlier
and their improved surveillance of the broad, flat knoll's crest. When

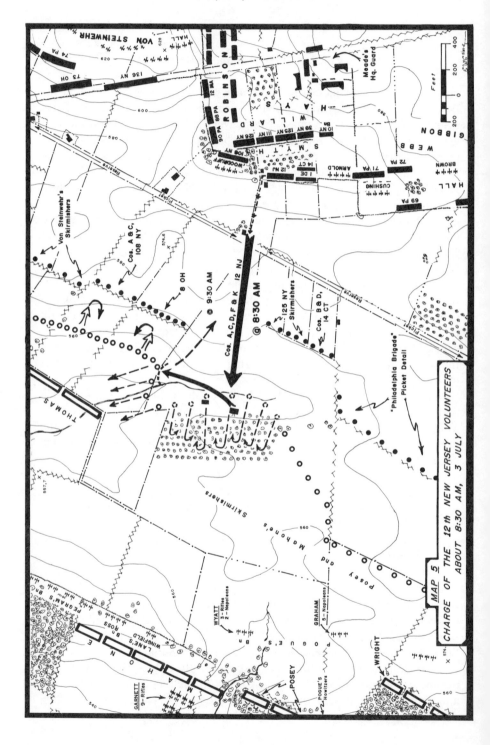

Feet

MAP 5

CHARGE OF THE 12th NEW JERSEY VOLUNTEERS
ABOUT 8:30 AM, 3 JULY

Sergeant Riley of Company K entered the barn, he saw some of the men poking the piles of hay and straw with their bayonets, searching for additional Rebel soldiers who may have been lurking about the stable area. However, only two Confederates were officially captured – one enlisted man and a major – though there may have been as many as four taken prisoner.[178]

Riley, who had witnessed the first attack of the 12th the previous afternoon, was nineteen when he enlisted as one of the original members of Company F in August 1862. During the Battle of Chancellorsville, he barely escaped serious injury when his blanket roll, tied to the top of his knapsack, was struck by an artillery shell. The impact ripped his blanket from its fastenings and severely shocked him. Additionally, his tin cup hanging from his haversack was pierced by a bullet.[179] Again, Riley was near the thick of the fight, but this time, he had a large barn to help protect him from any errant projectiles.

In the Bliss orchard, some Confederates hastily formed a new skirmish line. Though Captain Thompson commented that the barn was held "for some time," the Southern skirmishers soon rallied. In concert with some of Thomas' pickets, they began to ease their way back towards the buildings. This situation was confirmed when a small Union detachment was sent to investigate. The detail returned with "its commanding officer and others wounded" and reported that the "bushes [were] full of them."[180]

Meanwhile, inside the barn, Sergeant Riley climbed up and walked:

> on a joist, the flooring having been torn away, to a lattice window looking towards the Rebel lines where I had an excellent view, and saw a Reb officer trying to form and move forward a line of skirmishers. Only room for one to stand where I was. While I did the firing from there, others were loading and passing their guns to me. I had fired, perhaps some half dozen times or more when we heard them calling us from below. "Come down! come down quickly! They are trying to capture us!" And sure enough, on getting down and out, there to our right [north] could be seen coming what looked like a whole brigade.[181]

For Captain Thompson's detachment, then, the situation at the Bliss barn was deteriorating drastically, and to complicate matters:

> a battery which had been placed by the enemy in rear of the barn opened upon it with solid shot; stones fell in all

directions, and lime dust filled the air. The barn was no longer attractive as a summer resort.[182]

Riley expressed the same sentiment with the comment that there would be "no Libby (Prison) for us."[183] Thus, Thompson ordered a withdrawal.

This enemy activity did not go unnoticed by the men of the 8th Ohio, whose skirmish line was situated to the north-northeast of the Bliss barn. Captain David Lewis, Company G, "reported evidence of a strong force in a meadow below" their position on the western slope of the broad, flat knoll:

> Some 3-400 Rebels [rose] up but a few yards distance delivered their volley, rushed upon Captain Lewis with their bayonets.... [Lieutenant Colonel Sawyer with Captain William Kinney and his] Company B moved forward from the [Emmitsburg] road on a run, and... came over the crest.... [In the process Sawyer received] a ball through... his hat, which tore his hair and made an ugly wound.... [The force of the blow was enough to make Sawyer see] stars.[184]

With the bulk of the 8th Ohio thundering down the knoll's west slope, the Confederates who had been lurking about the bushes north of the Bliss buildings focused their attention on the Buckeyes to their front. The Southerners failed to watch Thompson's detail, then withdrawing under enemy artillery fire. Thompson's men moved by their right flank and fired a volley into the bushes.[185] The double Union threat of Jerseymen and Buckeyes, coupled with the small arms fire undoubtedly coming from Von Steinwehr's skirmish line to the northeast, and the effects of artillery fire, were too much for the Confederates. They retreated towards Stevens Run, "leaving several dead on the ground."[186]

As Thompson's troops withdrew, some men took time to gather up their wounded. As an occasional shell burst in his vicinity, Captain Azariah Z. Stratton checked the condition of the men who had fallen during their mad dash for the barn. Private Adams was dead. Stratton's older brother, "Henry," was able to stand, but could not walk. However, with the aid of a few comrades, Henry, along with "Will" Johnson, was carried back to Cemetery Ridge. Unfortunately, Henry died later that day.[187]

Indeed, the Civil War was devastating for the Strattons of Gloucester County, New Jersey. The Honorable Nathan T. Stratton, who had served as a U. S. Representative from 1850-1854, and his wife, Sarah, both merchants in Mullica Hill, must have been proud of their two sons though a bit apprehensive. During the summer of 1862, Edward L. Stratton, at the age of twenty-three, was instrumental in organizing Company F of the 12th New Jersey. He was eventually elected captain, and one of his enlistees was his nineteen year old brother, James. The following May, at Chancellorsville, Edward was seriously wounded, necessitating the amputation of a leg at the knee. Thirteen months after Gettysburg, James was killed at Ream's Station, near Petersburg.[188]

As Edward Stratton was recruiting men that fateful summer of 1862, news traveled to the small town of Swedesboro, five miles northwest of Mullica Hill. There, four of the five sons of farmer Emanuel and Elizabeth Stratton heeded the call for volunteers. The oldest brother, Emanuel, Jr., had the reputation of being the tallest man in Company F. During the Battle of Chancellorsville, he was shot in the chest. The ball passed down and lodged near his spine, causing temporarily paralysis and intense pain. He eventually received a medical discharge in March 1864. The next oldest enlistee, at the age of twenty-six, was mortally wounded in the charge for the Bliss barn. "Henry," described as being "of medium height, rugged health, and most intensely patriotic," left behind a widow and two children.[189]

Next in line was twenty-five year old Azariah, another organizer of Company F, who was promoted to captain after brother Edward was wounded. Azariah was the most fortunate of the four brothers; he was "never wounded enough to be off duty" and fought for the duration of the war.[190] However, the youngest of the quartet, Charles C. Stratton, barely sixteen when he enlisted, was killed in action at Spotsylvania Court House on 12 May 1864.[191]

Thus, over a two-year period, the Strattons of Mullica Hill and Swedesboro suffered three relatives killed, two seriously wounded and one only worse-for-the-wear. The devastation of families similar to the Strattons was repeated countless times on both sides during that bloody four-year war.

Private Adams, however, was alone as he met his maker that July morning. A farm boy from the small cross-roads community of Beverly, Gloucester County, he had enlisted at the age of nineteen in 1862. He was a large, spare young man:

> a boy of a quiet disposition who seemed to be old – much beyond his years, and not desirous of making many friends, or of participating in our sports or conversations; but minded his own business and attended strictly to duties, whilst his bravery was unquestioned.[192]

Possibly, Adams had some sixth sense that his mortal life would be short-lived.

Upon the return of Thompson's detail and the 8th Ohio, casualties were tabulated. The 12th had lost some twenty-eight men, and according to Captain Stratton, at least six of them were from Company F – four killed and two wounded. The 8th Ohio lost two men killed, including Sergeant John G. Peters of Company G, and eleven wounded.[193] No losses were reported by the 1st Delaware, for as Brady recalled, his detachment again retreated before reaching the farm buildings.[194] Confederate losses also were not reported in detail, though they probably were comparable to the number of Union casualties.

While the Union detachments were attempting to seize and hold the Bliss buildings, most of the Confederate army prepared for the upcoming artillery barrage and infantry assault on the Union center. The previous evening, the Southern artillery near McMillan Woods had been reinforced. According to Major William T. Poague:

> Late in the evening of the 2nd by... order... [of Colonel Walker] I reported to Major General Anderson for duty, and at last succeeded in getting ten of my guns into position. The balance (six howitzers) were kept a short distance in rear [near the northwest corner of Spangler's Woods], as no place could be found from which they could be used with advantage.[195]

Poague's artillery was further dispersed by the deployment of his remaining ten guns. Three rifled pieces of the Abermarle (Virginia) Artillery and two smoothbores of the Charlotte (North Carolina) Artillery, all under the command of Captain James W. Wyatt, were placed north of a timber or brush-covered hollow located between Spangler's and McMillan Woods. The remaining five smoothbores of the Madison (Mississippi) Light and Warrenton (Virginia) Artilleries, commanded by Captain George Ward, were posted on the south side of the hollow about 400 yards east of the crest of Seminary Ridge and near the northeast corner of Spangler's Woods.[196] Around 8:00 AM, as the Confederates listened to the sounds of battle floating across the fields, some of Poague's guns opened on the Union lines near the Copse of Trees:

> In the morning of the 3rd, while I [Poague] was at the position occupied by Captain Ward, the guns of Captain Wyatt opened on the enemy's position. In a few minutes the fire of several of their batteries was concentrated on these five guns.[197]

Captain Wyatt's cannoneers probably responded to the shelling of the Bliss Farmstead by Cushing's cannoneers, for during this exchange, Poague described the explosion of "a caisson of the enemy." These were Cushing's three limbers. In retaliation, Hazard's 2nd Corps artillery responded which resulted in Poague's order to Captain Wyatt to cease fire. Poague learned later that Wyatt allegedly had opened fire in compliance to an order received from A. P. Hill.[198]

As the artillery sparring subsided, the men of the 12th New Jersey charged the Bliss barn, and as the Federals solidified their position, Thomas' Brigade and Confederate skirmishers who been flushed out of the farm buildings counterattacked. This precipitated another exchange of artillery fire which subsided after the Jerseymen returned to Cemetery Ridge and Thomas' troops fell back to their positions along the Sunken Road. Meanwhile, additional cannons were repositioned. The nine rifled guns of Garnett's Battalion, under Major Richardson, were moved south from the vicinity of the McMillan House to a point on the left of Wyatt's command. There they were held in reserve on the reverse slope of the ridge.[199]

While the artillery prepared for the main Confederate attack, the infantry did not remain idle. That morning Posey reinforced his skirmish line near the Bliss buildings, for Sergeant Kirkpatrick of the 16th Mississippi wrote that his company was pressed into service once more:

> Our position is a little to the right of last evening –
> between the opposing batteries – in an open field exposed
> to shelling & to the hottest sun that ever shone on mortals.
> The quiet of the morning is broken about 9 AM by
> artillery. The sharpshooters had previously commenced
> plying their small arms, but the sun being so warm, they
> shoot lazily. Among the first shells that passed to and fro,
> one very unkindly carried away my gun and rendered it
> entirely unfit for service.[200]

As Kirkpatrick was sweltering under the hot sun, by mid-morning the Confederate pickets had re-occupied the Bliss buildings – the fourth time since the morning of 2 July. Southern sharpshooters resumed their harassing fire directed towards the main Union line. Just west of the Emmitsburg Road, Union skirmishers returned the enemy fire as they had done since sunrise. Chaplain Stevens observed the operations of the pickets and several years after the war wrote rather eloquently of the tense drama on the skirmish line:

Our picket reserve station was in the Emmitsburg Road in front of the regiment [opposite the Bliss barn]. The road was sunken nearly two feet, affording some protection at the fence. The picket line was at a fence about 200 yards in advance of the reserve, and the line of Rebel pickets about the same distance further on, some of it by the trees of the Bliss Orchard. Our men lay flat upon the ground by the fence hidden and somewhat protected by the posts and the lowest rails. Nothing was visible, usually to fire at, yet when any movement was apparent a shot or two would follow from vigilant watchers; then the rising rifle smoke would attract retaliating shots.[201]

At intervals, men on the skirmish line were relieved by soldiers from the picket reserve. In the open, flat farm lands between the lines, this process also was rather risky:

The relieving squad would leave the reserve rendezvous moving in any way possible to avoid the observation of the enemy, but when a place was reached where exposure was unavoidable each would take to running at highest speed, and upon reaching the fence would throw himself at once upon the ground. Then must the relieved ones get back to the reserve in a similar manner; and 'relieving' seemed a misnomer.... [However] not many of the runners were struck, for to hit such a rapidly moving object is a difficult feat....[202]

One of the Yankee skirmishers that morning was Sergeant E. B. Tyler of Company B, who several years after the war recounted his experiences:

We were stationed two or three fence lengths apart [about 30 to 40 feet] and... we could hardly see each other, ... the standing grain afforded considerable protection from view.... [We] occasionally spoke to one another on either hand for companionship or to ascertain if each was all right. [However there were some casualties.] A comrade, I think it was Hiram [H.] Fox, next to me on the left, said he had spoken to Corporal [Samuel G.] Huxam,... on the left, but obtained no reply. I suggested to him to crawl over... and see if all was right. [Fox] did so and reported back that Huxam was dead, shot through the head. He had evidently

66

become tired of lying flat upon the ground and firing through the lower rails, and risen up to a kneeling position and was aiming through the middle rails of the fence, a risk the Rebel sharpshooters had quickly availed themselves of, and not unlikely the very one that had attracted Huxam's attention was the one that proved too quick for him and fired the fatal shot.[203]

The skirmishers of the 14th Connecticut were not the only men on picket detail that morning. Near the Codori farm buildings, men of the Philadelphia Brigade harassed their Confederate counterparts. Also, near the Brian tenant house, the 2nd Delaware[204] supported by other details from Hays' Division, including men from the 125th New York of Willard's Brigade commanded by Captain Samuel C. Armstrong,[205] and companies A and C of the 108th New York, plied their trade.[206]

While the Federal skirmishers were choosing their targets, Confederate sharpshooters within the safety of the walls of the Bliss barn peppered the main Union line. About 10:00 AM the situation had become so intolerable that Captain Arnold told Chaplain Stevens that he had asked Colonel Smyth if the barn could be burned. According to Stevens, Smyth told Arnold that "the enemy would get behind the barn and do us more damage." Arnold replied that "the walls would be so hot men could not live in them."[207]

Nearby General Hays may have been entertaining the same thought, but he decided to try one more time to take and hold the Bliss Farm buildings. The task was assigned to Major Theodore G. Ellis and the men of the 14th Connecticut. Returning to his command, Ellis ordered Captain Samuel A. Moore to take charge of his Company F and three others of the "left wing" and prepare to advance his detachment.[208]

The thirty-two year old Ellis was a civil engineer from Hartford at the time of his enlistment. He was promoted to 1st lieutenant and later appointed the first adjutant of the regiment. When the New Englander reached Washington during the first week of September 1862, his abilities were desired by Brigadier General William H. French, then commander of the 3rd Division, Second Corps. Thus, Ellis was appointed acting assistant adjutant-general. Like many soldiers during the war, Ellis endured many medical ailments during his term of service. After the Battle of Fredericksburg, he suffered from swelling of the feet and legs. To compound this problem, he developed "remittent fever" which forced him to obtain a leave of absence by February 1863. Upon his recovery that spring, Ellis applied for the colonelcy of the 14th Connecticut, but General Hays denied it. Apparently, the decision disturbed Ellis, for two weeks later, by order of General Couch of the War Department, Ellis was listed as being absent without leave. Nonetheless, Ellis was exonerated and "released from the findings of the Military Commission" about the time he was promoted to major to date from 14 April 1863.[209]

Despite the misunderstandings with the army high command, Major Ellis had been described by a fellow soldier as being:

> thoughtful, accurate, and intelligent concerning his duties.... [The] men never doubted his thorough devotion to all and [his] position. His manner was genial and friendly towards those with which he had occasion to associate.... [H]is criticisms were often caustic, [but] just.[210]

Samuel A. Moore, a thirty year old resident of New Britain, Connecticut, was mustered into service as the 1st lieutenant of Company F, and after the Battle at Antietam, he was promoted to captain. When the army marched towards Falmouth on the north bank of the Rappahannock River, Moore was detailed to proceed to Washington to claim property that belonged to the regiment. In his absence, the 14th participated in the Battle of Fredericksburg:

> Upon returning [17 December]... and seeing only a little band left, scarcely one hundred fit for duty, – his feeling overpowered him, and for a while was completely overcome.[211]

Upon receiving the order from Ellis, Moore prepared his detachment, numbering only sixty men, for the 600 yard run to the Bliss barn. In his reminiscences, Reverend Stevens made a very pertinent observation:

> Why a force of only about half as large as either of the other parties previously sent for the same purpose was sent this time is one of the inscrutable things of the varying wisdom of war.[212]

Through attrition and casualties, by the summer of 1863, the 14th Connecticut was one of the smaller regiments in the Army of the Potomac. Including some forty men on the skirmish line, the unit numbered only 160 souls compared to the average size of a Union infantry regiment at Gettysburg of 300.[213] Stevens conjectured that the reason why so few men were assigned to retake the Bliss barn, was that someone "possibly...thought

68

that one Fourteenth man was equal to any two."[214] Realistically, one reason may have been that the men of Companies A and B were armed with the modern breech-loading Sharps rifles.[215]

Another probable explanation may have been the lack of timely intelligence reports available to Hays, Smyth, or Major Ellis concerning the enormity of the Confederate presence along Stevens Run and the Sunken Road north of the Bliss buildings – the area screened from their view by the broad, flat knoll. Though some of the skirmishers from Hays' Division, especially the 8th Ohio, were in a position to monitor the area for nearly eighteen hours, information on increased enemy activity may never have reached Cemetery Ridge. Following the proper military channels, any observations by Sawyer's 8th Ohio, technically, would be reported to the brigade commander, Colonel Carroll, and then to General Hays. Major Ellis then would receive the information from Hays via Colonel Smyth. However, the bulk of Carroll's Brigade had been detached and sent over to East Cemetery Hill the previous evening. Hence, Sawyer and his immediate superior were out of touch. Sawyer may have sent reports directly to General Hays, but if any were received, they were apparently not communicated to Smyth or Ellis prior to the advance of the left wing of the 14th Connecticut. Furthermore, though men of the 12th New Jersey had recently returned from the Bliss barn, documentation suggests that no one immediately communicated any reconnaissance information to Hays, Smyth or Ellis concerning the Confederates lurking below the knoll's crest.

However, if Hays was cognizant of the large Confederate presence near the Bliss Farm, why did he persist in sending small detachments to the area? Was Hays trying to avoid drawing too much attention that might precipitate a general engagement? Evidence indicates that Hays had been issued discretionary orders by Hancock concerning the destruction of the Bliss Farm. Sometime earlier on Cemetery Ridge, the two generals had been watching the fight for the farm buildings. Lieutenant Colonel C. H. Morgan, assistant inspector-general of the 2nd Corps, later reported that since the Confederates opposed the Federal occupation "so fiercely, [Hancock] ordered it burned lest General Hays should precipitate an engagement."[216] Though the time of Hancock's statement is not known, apparently Hays did not feel that a general brouhaha was forthcoming. During the morning of the third, he tried three times to capture and hold the Bliss Farm.

Whatever the situation was, with no current information of what lay ahead, Ellis detached only half of his available men to accomplish the task assigned. Possibly ignorant of the enemy's strength, Captain Moore's detachment was ushered around the Brian barn and down the farm lane to the Emmitsburg Road. As they passed by, General Hays shouted an order not to charge the barn in any compact formation; they were to "break and run," suggesting that Hays, by that time, had knowledge of the Confederate threat behind the broad, flat knoll. Upon crossing the roadway, the soldiers "were given orders to break and each man reach the barn as best he could."[217] As the Federals raced wildly for the Bliss barn, the abruptness of the attack forced the Confederate soldiers there to beat a hasty retreat for a fifth time:

> [T]he Rebels did not wait to greet their visitors, but "skedaddled"... out of the doors and other openings to take refuge in the orchard and house; the latter, which had not figured much in the former attacks now becoming quite formidable.[218]

One of the Union casualties in this charge was young, Private Thomas Jefferson Brainard of Company F:

> [He] was dashing ahead well to the front, and one of his comrades heard him shout to some who seemed laggard, "Come on you cowards!," when he was struck near his shoulder by a musket shot, the ball passing down into his chest.[219]

Nearby Captain John C. Broatch of Company A heard him yell and "leap into the air," and Sergeant-Major William B. Hincks, as he raced by, heard him cry out, "My God! my God! I'm hit O' how it hurts me!"[220]
Eventually Brainard:

> was borne to [Cemetery Ridge]... a little in rear of [the 14th Connecticut's position]. As soon as he saw us [Stevens] he called in a load voice, "O' Chaplain come here!" [I] hastened to him and dropping upon one knee at his side and took his hand. His frenzied grasp and the contortions of his... [face] told the agonies of pain he felt. Dr. [Frederick A.] Dudley came at once and probed the wound, but... [he gave] a significant glance which said, "Fatal, I leave him with you!" Wishing to draw him out, [I], still holding his hand and stroking his forehead, said, "What shall we think of you, Jeff?" With a startled expression he looked up, when seeming to comprehend the significance of the words and tone he spoke, "Tell my mother, tell – my —" and he was gone.[221]

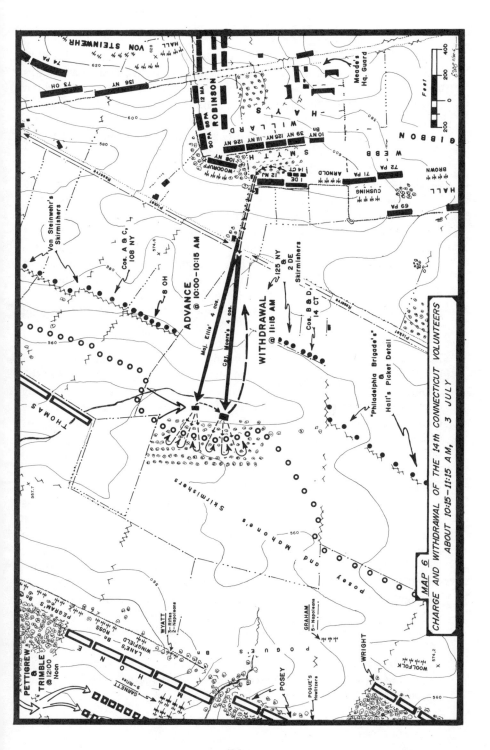

MAP 6

CHARGE AND WITHDRAWAL OF THE 14th CONNECTICUT VOLUNTEERS ABOUT 10:15–11:15 AM, 3 JULY

Brainard was a nineteen year old illiterate farm boy from Bloomfield, a small village located ten miles northwest of Hartford, Connecticut. With black hair, hazel eyes, and light complexion, "Little" Jeff's nickname was derived from his 5' 3 1/2" stature. He enlisted in 1862, and he probably felt that there was only one blemish to his military record. Shortly before the Gettysburg Campaign, on 31 May 1863, he was arrested "for not being on duty." However, no charges were officially filed. In defending the young private, Major Ellis stated that on the afternoon of 28 April 1863 a Captain Koon,* who was in temporary command of the regiment, had sent Jeff to check at brigade headquarters for "clothing that had been drawn for him and his company and that [he] did not get back in time and was not to blame."[222]

Though cleared, Brainard possibly felt that his integrity had been defamed in the eyes of his comrades. Therefore, two months later, he was at the head of a battalion, spurring the men forward and calling those cowards who appeared less than enthusiastic. Though his intentions were known only to him and his Maker, it is possible that Jeff believed that his honor and duty to his comrades-in-arms and to his country had been tarnished, thereby prompting him to take foolish risks in order to prove that he was a good soldier.[223]

As Brainard lay dying, Captain Moore and his sixty men entered the Bliss barn. The Confederates who had made good their escape now poured a withering small arms fire into the structure from two directions – the orchard and the house. The resulting crossfire made it difficult for anything in the open to survive. From Cemetery Ridge, Colonel Smyth and probably General Hays had been watching the developing situation. Realizing that Moore's detachment was outnumbered, Smyth sent word to Major Ellis to take the remaining four companies of the 14th Connecticut (except for the color guard) to re-enforce Moore's battalion, and drive the Confederates from the house. After crossing the Emmitsburg Road, Ellis led his men on a northerly route over the crest of the broad, flat knoll towards the Bliss house. However, this path took them closer to the main Confederate skirmish line near the Sunken Road. As Moore's detachment crossed the knoll's crest, his men suffered from a severe enfilade coming from Thomas' Brigade. "This flank fire could be termed volleys and several were hit by it," including men of Company I: 2nd Lieutenant Samuel H. Seward, "shot through the body," and 1st Lieutenant Frederick S. Seymour, "shot through the leg."[224] Upon reaching the house, a brief fire-fight occurred. First Lieutenant Henry P. Goddard recalled years later "how coolly [Sergeant J.]

---

* "Captain Koon" was not listed as an officer of the 14th Connecticut. See Adjutant General's Office, *Catalogue of Connecticut Volunteer Organizations, with Additional Enlistments and Casualties to July 1, 1864*, (Hartford: Case, Lockwood & Co., 1864), 491-525.

Sam[uel] Scranton [Company G] shot a Rebel in the doorway... as he would have shot a squirrel on his fathers farm."[225]   But some Confederates managed to fire a few parting rounds, mortally wounding Sergeant George W. Baldwin (Company I) and hitting Private John Fox (Company A) in the thigh.[226]

However, their stay in the Bliss house was short lived, for Ellis' men quickly realized that the home was a "poor place for protection." Due to the weatherboarded frame construction, the Minie balls were freely passing through the walls. Therefore, most of the New Englanders left the house for the safety of the stone and brick barn or the cover provided by a wood pile in the Bliss yard though the Confederate crossfire made the journey extremely hazardous.   Moreover, according to Stevens, as the 14th Connecticut consolidated their troops in the barn, a Confederate battery about 500 yards away, "in rear of the buildings,"[227] possibly Captain Wyatt's guns, opened fire.

The impromptu artillery fire created quite a stir along the Seminary Ridge line. To the south, Colonel Edward P. Alexander, then in charge of Longstreet's artillery, had been preparing for the bombardment that was to proceed Pickett's Charge.   However, after cannoneers fired on the 14th Connecticut during their occupation of the Bliss barn, the rest of A. P. Hill's artillery gradually commenced firing on the Union lines.   This rather annoyed Colonel Alexander, who recalled the situation that Friday forenoon some fourteen years later:

> About 11 AM the skirmishers in A. P. Hill's front got to fighting for a barn between the lines, and the artillery on both sides gradually took part until the whole of Hill's artillery in position, which I think was 63 guns, were heavily engaged for over a half an hour, but not one of the 75 guns which I... had in line was allowed to fire a shot, as we had at best a short supply of ammunition.... Gradually the cannonade... died out as it began and the field became nearly silent.[228]

To Alexander, the artillery fire was draining the supply of long-range ammunition that was essential for the upcoming cannonade or for any contingencies that might arise later.

When Confederate case shot and shell from A. P. Hill's artillery was directed towards the Bliss barn, and after Southern infantry recaptured the house, Major Ellis and his men determined that their position in the barn was untenable.   Enemy cannoneers soon found the range of the farm buildings, and a round crashed into the barn and exploded, killing Private

Moses G. Clement (Company G) while wounding several others. As Major Ellis recalled:

> [the] shell or projectile, entered the gable towards the house [north side] and burst inside.... The projectile was probably fired by the "rebs" as it contained grape shot which was not used by our artillery. One of the shot was picked up and shown me.[229]

With the debris flying about Sergeant Julius W. Knowlton "received 'a welt'... that nearly broke his back."[230]

As the Confederate rounds pelted the farmstead, their sharpshooters also were hitting their marks. Amid the tempest, one soldier, Corporal Thomas W. Gardner (Company H), had been firing out of one of the barn windows when a Confederate bullet struck him and "plowed a permanent furrow along the top of his head."[231] Nearby, 2nd Lieutenant John A. Tibbets (Company F) "swore at the Johnnies for wounding him in his sound arm."[232]

Nevertheless, several of the New Englanders were good marksmen. Private Blackford Benson of the 1st South Carolina Regiment wrote that they:

> had it hot. The Yankee skirmishers charged us several times.... They took possession of a large barn to our right and commenced firing from the windows. The first shot killed Sergt. Rhoades. Our flank being exposed, our artillery fired the barn.[233]

Nearby was Thomas M. Littlejohn of the 13th South Carolina, who wrote after the war that "one man was killed by a sharpshooter [firing] from a dwelling house in what is now an apple orchard."[234] He was undoubtedly referring to the Bliss house and orchard.

As the noon hour approached, the situation looked very grim for the men of the 14th Connecticut. The Bliss Farm fighting was escalating into a major clash of arms. The struggle involved not only skirmishers but a sizable portion of the Confederate artillery whose fire created a disruptive atmosphere along the Union main line. About 11:30 AM, General Hays prepared to execute Hancock's discretionary order to torch the Bliss buildings.

Near the Brian house, the men of the 111th New York Regiment of Willard's Brigade were posted behind a stone wall along the eastern edge of the Brian orchard. Among them was Sergeant Charles A. Hitchcock,

Company G. In a letter written some twenty-three years later, Hitchcock claimed that as he was "sitting on the ground eating hardtack," he overheard General Hays mention to Colonel McDougall of the 111th that a volunteer was needed to carry an order out to the Bliss barn:

> I looked around to see if anyone was going as McDougall repeated the order or request in a loud voice. As none appeared to volunteer, I got up [and] told the [general] I would go.... [Hays] specified the orders to me which I was to carry to the officer in command... [at the barn. After he gathered some matches and paper, he started on his mission] at a double quick.[235]

Meanwhile, possibly General Hays had second thoughts about sending only one courier through the storm of shot and shell. A mounted messenger was dispatched to insure the order would reach Major Ellis, and for this task Captain James Parke Postles of Smyth's staff volunteered.

Enlisting at Wilmington on 7 August 1861, Postles had been appointed 1st Lieutenant of Company A, 1st Delaware. At the Battle of Antietam, where he was slightly wounded, he received a promotion to captain on 18 September 1862. Though Postles' health began to fail from chronic diarrhea, eventually, on 9 March 1863, Colonel Smyth appointed him as his acting assistant inspector-general.[236]

Some forty years after the battle, Postles wrote of his ride out to the Bliss barn:

> [I] rode off slowly down the [Brian] lane, passed a little frame building [Brian tenant house] and crossed the Emmitsburg Road; and on reaching the field beyond, I put my horse into a gentle lope. As soon as I crossed the... [road], the enemy in the house opened fire on me, which grew hotter and hotter as I drew near... till it was a constant wonder and surprise to me that none of the bullets, which I heard whistling around and so close to me, had hit me.... It immediately flashed upon me that my only chance of safety was in keeping my horse in motion....[237]

As he reached the barn, Postles dug his spurs into the horse's sides and pulled back on the reins with all his weight in order to keep the beast dancing in a stationary position. He delivered his message "at the top of [his] voice, so the enemy could hear as well [as they] were firing at [him] from every door and window of the house."[238] Close by, Corporal Orsamus

B. Sawyer (Company A) heard Postles bellow, "Colonel Smyth orders you to burn the house and barn and retire."[239] Probably Sergeant Hitchcock arrived about this time with the same directive.[240]

After Major Ellis acknowledged the receipt of the order, Postles:

> loosened my bridle reins, still holding my spurs into the horse's sides and the poor brute sped away, almost as though shot out of a gun. When I had gotten about three hundred yards away, beginning to feel quite safe again, I turned in my saddle and taking off my cap, shook it at [the Confederates] in defiance.[241]

For his ride, Captain Postles was awarded the Medal of Honor on 18 July 1892 "for conspicuous gallantry at the Battle of Gettysburg."[242]

As Postles galloped back towards Cemetery Ridge, the Connecticut men prepared to execute the order and to extricate themselves from the Bliss barn. Accompanied by some men of Company A, Ellis sprinted over to the house which now had apparently been vacated by the Confederates who had tried their best to pick off Captain Postles. Once there, Ellis supervised the removal of the dead and wounded and gave instructions to the men to torch the dwelling. Private James A. Stroazzi recalled that some men went from room to room setting bedding materials on fire. Then they returned to the barn, dodging bullets as they ran.[243] While Ellis' detail went to the house, others busied themselves in the barn by igniting the piles of hay and straw. When Ellis' detail returned, Sergeant Albert A. DeForest and some of the men approached Adjutant Frederick B. Doten with a special request. They had captured some of Mr. Bliss' chickens and asked for permission to take them back to the main line. Ellis wrote after the war that permission "was upon this occasion granted."[244]

As the men from Connecticut fell back towards Cemetery Ridge, the hopes and dreams of William Bliss and his family were consumed in flames. The buildings – whose walls had been silent witnesses to six years of fond memories and hard work – had sheltered soldiers from such divergent parts of the country as Mississippi and Connecticut, and had withstood approximately thirty hours of shot and shell. They were destroyed in a matter of minutes.

Reaching the area just west of the Emmitsburg Road, opposite the Brian tenant house, where the terrain shielded them from the small arms fire, the 14th Connecticut rallied. The outfit was exhausted from their ordeal in the hot, humid weather. About 200 yards away, Sergeant Hitchcock was just returning from his mission when he was stopped by General Hays. After informing his division commander that he had "executed" his order, Hays assigned Hitchcock additional duties. Observing that the men of the 14th Connecticut were not assembling at the proper place, Hitchcock was ordered to "go down there... and halt them at that place [Brian tenant house]." A short time later, Ellis' command recuperated from their ordeal in the shade of some trees about the old house, trying "to catch breath and to shake the terrific thirst at a well." There, Hitchcock and the Connecticut men remained for nearly an hour. However, the sergeant "began to feel lonesome away from [his] company and hungry as usual.... Seeing no use to [his] staying there," Hitchcock returned to his unit with Hays' permission. Eventually, the 14th Connecticut rejoined its color guard which was still in position behind the 1st Delaware on Cemetery Ridge.[245]

As the men withdrew from the burning buildings and a relative quiet began to return to the fields south of Gettysburg, the Confederates behind Seminary Ridge were completing preparations for Pickett's Charge. The brigades of Heth's Division, now under the command of Brigadier General James Johnston Pettigrew, were shifted to the area just south of McMillan Woods when the men of Scales' and Lanes' Brigades under Major General Isaac Trimble came into line. To the south, amongst the trees of Spangler's Woods, the Virginians of Pickett's Division marshalled.

On Cemetery Ridge some soldiers took the opportunity during the cessation of hostilities to eat what little they could scrounge up. Bliss' chickens began stewing in makeshift pots of the 14th Connecticut[246] while the bones of those unfortunate fowl absconded the day before lay strewn about the area of the 12th New Jersey near the Brian barn. This lull, however, was broken about 1:00 PM when the Confederate artillery bombardment began. As shells crashed around the Union center, the artillerymen of the 2nd Corps, along with others from Cemetery Hill to Little Round Top, responded to the Confederate challenge.

Though the activities around the Bliss Farm were quickly overshadowed by Pickett's Charge, the smoldering ruins of the buildings, the ten-acre orchard, and the numerous fence lines that remained intact, were to play a part in the assault by the commands of Pettigrew and Trimble – the farm, with its many obstacles, laid directly in their paths. As the long, gray lines moved forward shortly after 3:00 PM, the Union artillery remained relatively silent. However, according to Brigadier General Joseph R. Davis in his official report, after his brigade reached a "strong post and rail fence about three-quarters of a mile from the enemy's position" (the fence line marking the western boundary of the Bliss property), the Yankee gunners opened with "a heavy fire of grape, canister, and shell." Situated near the center of Pettigrew's battle line, Davis' advance "was interrupted by other fences of a similar character, in crossing which the alignment [of the

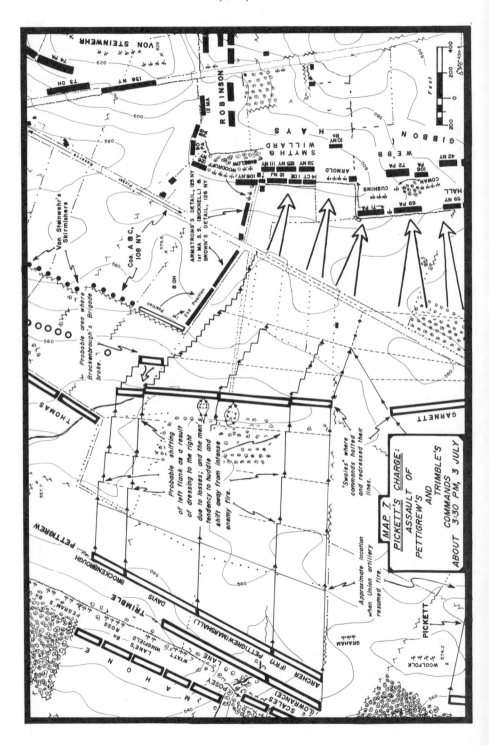

MAP 7

PICKETT'S CHARGE:
ASSAULT OF
PETTIGREW'S
AND
TRIMBLE'S
COMMANDS
ABOUT 3:30 PM, 3 JULY

brigade] became more or less deranged."[247] Though Davis did not mention much concerning the advance itself, the center and left flank units of Pettigrew's line had to pass through the Bliss orchard, around the smoldering ruins of the farm buildings, and across any fences that remained standing. These obstructions would certainly "derange" Davis' advancing troops.

Crossing the lands of William Bliss, the effects of the artillery fire on the Southern battle lines and the method of closing ranks were critical to the events that were to follow. In his work on Pickett's Charge, George R. Stewart indicated that the right flanks of Pettigrew's and Trimble's commands marched in a straight line for approximately 1,000 yards. Possibly, the Confederate right followed an established fence line. This fence extended from a point near the northwest corner of Spangler's Woods, along the southern boundary of the Bliss property, to a point on the Emmitsburg Road about 300 yards north of the Codori farm house.[248] As the Confederates moved forward, their lines had a stable right flank. Davis indicated in his report that "the order had been given that...the division would attack the enemy's batteries, keeping dressed to the right."[249] Consequently, as the soldiers were blown or knocked out of the ranks by the Yankee artillery fire, the left flanks of Pettigrew's and Trimble's commands shifted to the right, or south, thereby producing a gap between Pettigrew's left flank unit, Colonel John M. Brockenbrough's Brigade, and the right flank of Thomas' command at the southern end of the Sunken Road. This progressively widening gap made it increasingly difficult for the skirmishers of Thomas' Brigade to support the advance and protect the flank of Brockenbrough's line. As the Southerners approached from the west, it appeared to the men of the 8th Ohio that the Southerners were executing a right oblique maneuver. Meanwhile, a gap in the Confederate line widened to the right front of the Buckeyes.

Upon reaching the area of Stevens Run, just east of the Bliss ruins, Pettigrew halted his division to redress his lines. However, the Confederates found no respite from the Union fire. Additionally, Brockenbrough's men had to cope with the 8th Ohio in their immediate front on the western slope of the broad, flat knoll. With the increased pressure created by the Buckeyes, Brockenbrough's Brigade, which had suffered severely on 1 July, broke and fell back towards Seminary Ridge. This further widened the gap between Pettigrew's left and the Confederates posted in the Sunken Road. Thomas's troops now found it nearly impossible to support the advancing gray lines, and this permitted the 8th Ohio and other Yankee troops to enfilade Pettigrew's line.

By 5:00 PM Pickett's Charge and the Battle of Gettysburg was history. As the sun sank lower in the western sky, it became obscured by dark, ominous clouds that indicated the approach of rainstorms. The boom of artillery was soon replaced by the crack of lightning. Still, the Bliss Farm caused some minor problems. To remedy the situation, men of the 1st Delaware were given the task of chasing some Confederates away from the ruins of the Bliss buildings.[250] The morrow was Independence Day.

Chapter Five

"TOO BAD, OH, TOO BAD!"

During the evening of the third and much of the fourth it rained heavily, as if Mother Nature attempted to wash the crimson plains of Gettysburg clean after three days of bloodletting. As the eastern sky grew brighter on that Independence Day, both armies stared across the shell-torn no man's land, part of which had been the happy home of the Bliss family, and wondered what the gray day would bring.

By dawn both commanders had assessed the damage done to their respective commands. During the seventy-two hours of the Battle of Gettysburg, 160,000 Americans fought over approximately twenty-five square miles of Adams County countryside. In the process, over 51,000 soldiers were listed as either being killed, wounded, or missing. But what were the cold, impersonal statistics for the thirty-two hours of the Bliss Farm struggle and how did they compare to the overall battle?

The Bliss Farm engagements consisted of a series of small scale skirmishes, involving hundreds of men at any given moment, during which the farm buildings changed hands at least <u>ten times</u>. Though numbers and losses are difficult to compile due to the poor record keeping of the era, an estimate of those totals can be made by examining the returns in the *Official Records*, various regimental histories, personal accounts, and other scholarly works. Between sunrise of 2 July and the early afternoon of 3 July, approximately 2,160 Union and 2,310 Confederate soldiers fought around the Bliss Farm, suffering casualties of about 360 and 470, respectively. The Southern troops suffered a slightly higher percentage loss – 20% versus 17% (See Appendix B). When the Bliss Farm figures are compared to the overall numbers and losses of the battle, they account for only 2.8% of the men engaged and about 2% of the casualties.

As for the William Bliss family, of all the civilians that had been directly affected by Lee's Gettysburg Campaign, they were the only ones who had lost nearly everything except for the clothes on their back and what

81

little they were able to haul away. The Bliss family was confronted with seemingly impossible burdens to overcome, both financially and spiritually:

> The daughter of Mr. Bliss [possibly Frances] writes [to Chaplain Stevens] that when the family returned to their place... most of the wall of the barn was standing, though "all the woodwork was burned out," and the house was entirely destroyed.[251]

Returning to Chautauqua County, New York by 1867, the Blisses spent the rest of their lives attempting to collect reparations from government agencies for the destruction of their farm. None were ever received (See Appendix F).

Beyond the tragic loss of life and the unfortunate destruction of the Bliss property, the actions around the farm were significant. In retrospect, the Bliss Farm skirmishes, which have never been analyzed, had a direct bearing on the battle's outcome.

On 2 July, regardless of the delay of the Confederate attacks, the lack of their coordination and the unpredictability of several Union officers, the Southerners nearly cracked the Federal positions along Cemetery Ridge. Lee's plan may have met with greater success if the prescribed strategy could have been maintained. However, due in part to the breakdown of the en echelon attacks, the Confederates were unable to sustain a constant pressure on the Federal positions from the Copse of Trees to Culp's Hill. Thus Ewell's troops alone assailed East Cemetery Hill, holding onto a portion of that summit for a few precious and critical minutes before the arrival of Yankee re-enforcements from Carroll's Brigade.

One of the keys to a potential Confederate victory on 2 July was the maintenance of the en echelon attack plan. However, the lack of A. P. Hill's attention to his corps' combat operations and the importance that Anderson and Posey gave to the tactical situation at the Bliss Farm were the catalysts that spurred its dissolution.

Unfortunately for Lee, A. P. Hill uncharacteristically was not involved in his corps' operations on 2 July. Although the former commander of the famous Light Division had saved the day at Antietam ten months earlier, he, nevertheless, remained passive at Gettysburg. According to one biographer, Hill, "assigned to a cooperative role, ... never seemed to get caught in the fever of battle."[252] To Hill, the tardiness of Longstreet's attacks on 2 July may have reminded him of the Battles of Mechanicsville and Frayser's Farm during the Seven Days' Battles a year earlier. During those battles, delays by Jackson had cost the Confederates resounding victories. As the sun rose in the Pennsylvania skies, apparently Hill's enthusiasm melted away with the rising temperature and humidity. As the battle evolved that afternoon, Hill's inactive role in translating Lee's strategy to his division commanders left R. H. Anderson in an uncomfortable position.

Mary Boykin Chestnut, a childhood playmate of Anderson's and later one of the most famous diarists of the Civil War South, wrote that he was "silent but discreet."[253] Apparently this trait of discreetness remained with Anderson during the rest of his life. Moreover, while serving as an instructor and on frontier duty, he became meditative and developed a fondness for solitary strolls.[254] Douglas Southall Freeman described Anderson as:

> [a] modest gentleman... easygoing [and] generous.... Anderson never was disposed to quibble over authority or to indulge in any sort of boastfulness. Already he was beloved in the Army for his kindness, his amiability and his unselfishness.[255]

However, in assessing Anderson's performances prior to Gettysburg, Freeman noted several potentially critical problems with the South Carolinian's approach to command. At Williamsburg, Virginia, Freeman believed that Anderson was "not altogether careful in reconnaissance... [and he was] possibly a bit negligent in watching small details."[256] Freeman also suggested that Anderson may have excelled earlier in the war due to the guiding hand of his West Point classmate James Longstreet.[257] According to Anderson's biographer, in any personal confrontation Anderson was guided by his own brand of ethics based on the Scriptures. For minor infractions – forgive and forget. If he had to reprimand someone, he did it in private to prevent embarrassing that person in front of his peers. Seldom did Anderson go to others with his problems until he had exhausted all other avenues. With greater misconduct, he consulted with a personal confidant such as Longstreet.[258] Thus Longstreet probably knew how to handle his old friend to maximize his potential. Likewise, Anderson considered him a confidant.

However, with the reorganization of the Army of Northern Virginia after Chancellorsville, the well-tuned working relationship between Longstreet and Anderson was dissolved. Anderson's Division was transferred to Hill's Corps. A. P. Hill was not acquainted with Anderson and would not know how best to deal with him. Conversely, Anderson probably did not feel comfortable confiding in Hill during the battle. Thus Anderson's solitary approach to problem solving may have manifested itself at the critical moment when the en echelon attacks on the Union center were showing signs of disintegration.

In their official reports on Gettysburg, Hill and Anderson acknowledged their roles in the en echelon attack. Hill wrote:

> General Longstreet was to attack the left flank of the enemy, ... and I was to cooperate with him with such of my brigades from the right as could join in with his troops in the attack.[259]

Likewise, Anderson indicated that he:

> was... ordered to put the troops of my division into action by brigades as soon as those of General Longstreet's Corps had progressed so far in their assaults as to be connected with my right flank.[260]

However, the en echelon strategy was altered by the time it reached brigade command level. Possibly Anderson, his staff, his brigade and/or his regimental commanders did not appreciate the importance of their roles in the plan. Posey reported that he had received an order from Anderson indicating he was to advance after General Wright. A second order received through Captain Shannon, one of Anderson's staff officers, altered the first. Though the text and content of this second order has not survived, its results have been documented. Posey initially ordered the advance of only his "right two regiments," and Colonel Harris of the 19th Mississippi (Posey's Brigade) wrote that he was to advance only his right wing. These facts suggest that, in the second order, Anderson may have altered the basic en echelon plan, or that it was changed by Shannon and/or Posey.

A review of the military record of Captain Shannon hints that he had some problem during his military service, especially after Gettysburg. For unknown reasons, he might have lost the desire to fulfill his military commitment. Shannon's service record casts doubts concerning his reliability as an aide.[261] Thus, Shannon may have garbled Anderson's second order to Posey.

However, an analysis of available data suggests an additional scenario. During the afternoon of 2 July, Anderson probably viewed the continued, harassing fire of the Federal skirmishers occupying the Bliss Farm to his left front as a serious threat to his division's continued participation in the en echelon offensive. Yankees holding a commanding position halfway between the opposing lines would pose a serious threat to the left flank of Wright's Brigade as it advanced in support of the brigades led by Wilcox and Perry. An enfilade coming from the vicinity of the Bliss buildings, therefore, threatened the success of the assaults by Anderson's right three brigades and of the en echelon plan. To insure success, the Bliss Farm threat had to be neutralized.

However, any change in the prescribed attack plan, theoretically, would have to have been cleared with Anderson's superior. But, Hill was not actively involved in his corps' combat operations that day. Thus Anderson, without guidance from corps command and isolated from anyone with whom he could discuss his problems, was forced to deal alone with the pressures of a complicated and critical situation. His five brigades were stretched over nearly a mile of undulating terrain – from McMillan Woods to the area just south of Spangler's Woods. The troops of Wilcox and Perry were engaged in a desperate struggle along the Emmitsburg Road, and Wright's Brigade was preparing to advance to their support. Thus the apprehensive Anderson issued to Posey an order which may have been discretionary in nature. Possibly Posey was instructed to clear the Yankees away from the Bliss Farm in a manner that would not draw too much attention from the main Union line prior to the main Confederate assault in that sector.

Posey's piecemeal deployment of his Mississippians may have been a ruse to flush the Yankees away from the Bliss buildings. Possibly the advance of Posey's "right two regiments," (which according to Harris of the 19th Mississippi, halted at their skirmish line) and the subsequent attack of the Baker's 16th (the brigade's left-center), was designed as a possible encircling maneuver. The Federal skirmishers, threatened by the bulk of the 48th and 19th Mississippi to their left-front, may have been compelled to retire when faced with the assault of the 16th Mississippi to their front. However, Anderson and Posey had not anticipated the Federal response – the attack of the 8th Ohio, 12th New Jersey, and the 106th Pennsylvania.

The result of Posey's attempt to clear the farmstead of Yankee skirmishers sealed the fate of the en echelon plan. The Yankee counterstroke, in part, resulted in the deployment of the 8th Ohio on the crest of the broad, flat knoll. Later, at the critical moment when the Mississippians were needed to maintain the en echelon assaults and support Wright's attack on the Union center, half of Posey's command was pinned down by the enfilade coming from the Buckeyes.

As the situation deteriorated that afternoon, Anderson may have become flustered and thought that the unexpected Yankee counterthrust was the beginning of a major attack. Adjusting to this new potential threat, Anderson may have personally rescinded an earlier order sent via Captain Shannon and ordered Mahone to remain on Seminary Ridge and support the artillery. Thus Posey was denied his much needed support. Anderson's concentration on the Bliss Farm situation, then, could explain the observations of Wilcox's adjutant-general. After the battle, Wilcox described the incident to Lee:

> When I sent my Adjutant General back to the Division commander asking that he send me re-enforcements, ... my Adj't Gen'l returned and reported that General Anderson said 'Tell Gen'l Wilcox to hold his own, that things will change;' that he found Gen'l A. back in the woods which were in rear [west] of the Emmitsburg Road several hundred yards in a ravine,* his horse tied and all his staff lying on the ground (indifferent) as tho' nothing was going on.... I am quite certain that Gen'l A. never saw a foot of the ground on which his three brigades fought on the 2nd July.... Captain Shannon, Aide to Gen'l A., told me, that he did (however) go to Gen'l Mahone with an order from Gen'l A. to advance, and that Gen'l Mahone refused to move, stating that Gen'l A. had told him to hold that position, but says the aide, I am just from Gen'l A. and he orders you to advance. No, says Mahone, I have orders from Gen'l A. himself to remain here, and did not move.[262]

Another consequence of the Federals strongly re-enforcing their skirmish line on the broad, flat knoll was that it prevented Posey's left wing and at least part of Pender's Division from advancing on Cemetery Hill. By 7:00 PM, when Thomas' and Perrin's Brigades advanced to the Sunken Road just west of Stevens Run, they were faced with a heavy Yankee picket force aligned upon a commanding rise. With the retreat of Wright's and part of Posey's Brigades to the south, that Yankee picket line became virtually impregnable. Finally, the breakdown in communications due to inadequate staff work following the untimely loss of Pender added to the confusion.

All these factors prevented a sustained Confederate attack on the Yankee line between the Copse of Trees and Culp's Hill. Thus the Southerners were prevented from marshaling major assaults on three slopes of Cemetery Hill, ironically the weakest spot on the Union line during the late afternoon and early evening hours of 2 July. If the en echelon plan was maintained, Carroll's Brigade and the remnants of Robinson's Division

---

* Though the exact location of this "ravine" is not known, there are two possibilities: a low area near the southern edge of Spangler's Woods just west of the Spangler farm buildings near Wilcox's position, or the low area situated about half way between Spangler's and McMillan Woods near the Bliss Farm and Mahone's position.

would not have been sufficient reserves to stop the converging attacks of Hill's and Ewell's Confederates on Cemetery Hill.

It is debatable, given the existing troop dispositions, whether the Confederates could have captured and held Cemetery Hill had they retained the integrity of the en echelon plan. Elements of the Union 6th Corps probably would have been available to attempt to retake the hill. However, Southern troops would have had the opportunity to retain a sheltered position behind the broad, flat knoll only 600 yards from the main Yankee line.

The Bliss Farmstead, which proved to be such a critical area during the 2 July fighting, continued to plague the Confederates on 3 July. The attacks of the 12th New Jersey and the 14th Connecticut that morning precipitated several impromptu artillery exchanges. These bombardments wasted precious long-range ammunition that Colonel E. P. Alexander and other Confederate artillerists desperately needed three hours later when they attempted to soften the Union center and to support advancing Confederate infantry. Additionally, the retention of the Buckeyes' advanced positions on the broad, flat knoll was devastating during Pickett's Charge. The effects of the Union artillery, exacerbated by the Buckeyes' heavy small arms fire, forced the withdrawal of Brockenbrough's Brigade and prevented Thomas and other commands of A. P. Hill's Corps from supporting the left flanks of Pettigrew and Trimble. If the Confederates could have gained control of the knoll the previous evening, Thomas, Perrin, and other brigades of Pender's Division would have been in a better position to support Pettigrew's and Trimble's left, thereby preventing a Yankee enfilade.

Undoubtedly, the fight over the Bliss Farm affected the outcome of the battle. But to proclaim a Southern victory had certain events transpired differently would be difficult to say. However, the Confederate cause certainly would have had a better chance if the Bliss Farm had not existed. With no substantial cover between the lines, both sides would not have concentrated so much time and effort to try and hold buildings. The Southerners would have focused their attention on sustaining the en echelon attack on 2 July, and may have, at the every least, temporarily captured Cemetery Hill, if not force a Union retreat. If the Yankee lines held, with the Confederates controlling the broad, flat knoll, Pickett's Charge on the third may have met with greater success.

Perhaps the results of the battle would have been the same, but undoubtedly at a higher cost in casualties, some which may have had serious consequences. Junior officers such as General Alexander Hays or "Scrappy Little Billy" Mahone, or even A. P. Hill, key figures in subsequent campaigns, may have been wounded or killed. Such theoretical losses may have affected the course of the war similar to the loss of Stonewall Jackson after Chancellorsville. What effects those losses would have had on the war efforts, both North and South, can only be contemplated by "Monday morning quarterbacks" and "arm chair" generals who are constantly seeking more fodder to play the "what if" games of Gettysburg.

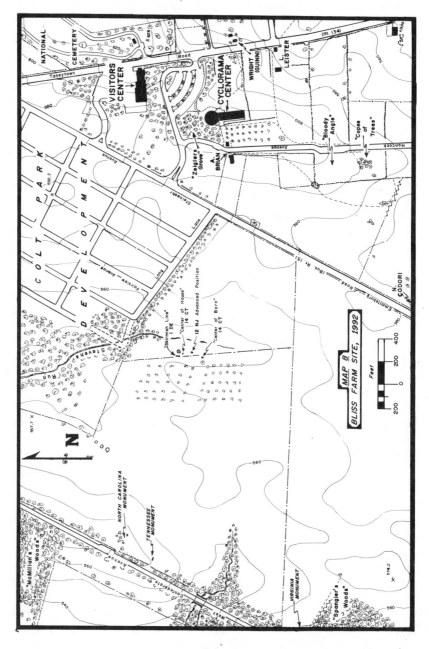

Appendix A

ORDER OF BATTLE
TROOPS INVOLVED IN THE BLISS
FARM STRUGGLE

ARMY OF THE POTOMAC
Major General George G. Meade

2ND CORPS
Major General Winfield S. Hancock
Brigadier General John Gibbon

2ND DIVISION
Brigadier General John Gibbon
Brigadier General William Harrow

2nd Brigade
Brigadier General Alexander S. Webb

69th Pennsylvania Regiment
Colonel Dennis O'Kane
Captain William Davis

72nd Pennsylvania Regiment
Colonel DeWitt C. Baxter
Lieutenant Colonel Theodore Hesser

71st Pennsylvania Regiment
Colonel Richard P. Smith

106th Pennsylvania Regiment
Lieutenant Colonel William L. Curry

3RD DIVISION
Brigadier General Alexander Hays

1st Brigade
Colonel Samuel S. Carroll

14th Indiana Regiment
Colonel John Coons

4th Ohio Regiment
Lieutenant Colonel Leonard W. Carpenter

8th Ohio Regiment
Lieutenant Colonel Franklin Sawyer

7th West Virginia Regiment
Lieutenant Colonel Jonathan H. Lockwood

2nd Brigade
Colonel Thomas A. Smyth
Lieutenant Colonel Francis E. Pierce

14th Connecticut Regiment
Major Theodore G. Ellis

1st Delaware Regiment
Lieutenant Colonel Edward P. Harris
Captain Thomas B. Hizar
Lieutenant William Smith
Lieutenant John T. Dent

12th New Jersey Regiment
Major John T. Hill

10th New York Regiment
Major George F. Hopper

108th New York Regiment
Lieutenant Colonel Francis E. Pierce

3rd Brigade
Colonel George L. Willard
Colonel Eliakim Sherrill
Lieutenant Colonel James M. Bull

39th New York Regiment
Major Hugo Hildebrandt

111th New York Regiment
Colonel Clinton MacDougal
Lieutenant Colonel Isaac M. Luck
Captain Aaron P. Seeley

125th New York Regiment
Lieutenant Colonel Levin Crandell

126th New York Regiment
Colonel Eliakim Sherrill
Lt. Colonel James M. Bull

Appendix A

Unattached

1st Company, Massachusetts Sharpshooters
Captain William Plummer
Lieutenant Emmerson Bicknell

Artillery Brigade
Captain John G. Hazard

Battery B, 1st New York Light
Artillery
(14th New York Battery Attached)
Captain James B. Rorty
Lieutenant Robert E. Rodgers
Lieutenant Albert S. Sheldon

Battery A, 1st Rhode Island Light
Artillery
Captain William A. Arnold

Battery B, 1st Rhode Island Light
Artillery
Lieutenant T. Fred Brown
Lieutenant William S. Perrin

Battery I, 1st U. S. Artillery
Lieutenant George A. Woodruff
Lieutenant Tully McCrea

Battery A, 4th U. S. Artillery
Lieutenant Alonzo H. Cushing
Sergeant Frederick Fuger

ARMY OF NORTHERN VIRGINIA
Lieutenant General Robert E. Lee

THIRD CORPS
Lieutenant General Ambrose P. Hill

ANDERSON'S DIVISION
Major General Richard H. Anderson

Posey's Brigade	*Mahone's Brigade*
Brigadier General Carnot Posey	Brigadier General William Mahone
12th Mississippi Regiment	6th Virginia Regiment
Colonel William H. Taylor	Colonel George T. Rodgers
16th Mississippi Regiment	12th Virginia Regiment
Colonel Samuel E. Baker	Lieutenant Colonel Everard M. Field
19th Mississippi Regiment	16th Virginia Regiment
Colonel Nathaniel H. Harris	Lieutenant Colonel Joseph H. Ham
48th Mississippi Regiment	41st Virginia Regiment
Colonel Joseph M. Jayne	Colonel William A. Parkam
	61st Virginia Regiment
	Colonel Virginius D. Groner

Lane's Artillery Brigade
(Sumter *Georgia* Artillery)
Major John Lane

Company (Battery) A
Captain Hugh M. Ross

Company (Battery) C
Captain John T. Wingfield

Wright's Brigade
Brigadier General Ambrose R. Wright

2nd Georgia Battalion
Major George W. Ross
Captain Charles J. Moffett

3rd Georgia Regiment
Colonel Edward J. Walker

22nd Georgia Regiment
Colonel Joseph A. Wasden
Captain B. C. McCurry

48th Georgia Regiment
Colonel William Gibson
Captain M. R. Hall

HETH'S DIVISION
Major General Henry Heth

Garnett's Artillery Battalion
Lieutenant Colonel John J. Garnett

Donaldsonville (Louisiana) Artillery
Captain Victor Maurin

Norfolk (Virginia) Artillery
Captain Joseph D. Moore

Norfolk Light Artillery Blues
Captain Charles R. Grandy

Pittsylvania (Virginia) Artillery
Captain John W. Lewis

Appendix A

PENDER'S DIVISION
Major General William D. Pender
Brigadier General James H. Lane

1st (McGowan's) Brigade
Colonel Abner Perrin

1st South Carolina (Orr's) Rifles
Captain William H. Hadden

1st South Carolina Regiment
Major. Charles W. McCreary

12th South Carolina Regiment
Colonel John L. Miller

13th South Carolina Regiment
Lieutenant Colonel Benjamin T.
Brockman

14th South Carolina Regiment
Lieutenant Colonel Joseph N. Brown

2nd Brigade
Brigadier General James H. Lane
Colonel Clark M. Avery

7th North Carolina Regiment
Captain J. McLeod Turner
Captain James C. Harris

18th North Carolina Regiment
Colonel John D. Barry

28th North Carolina Regiment
Colonel Samuel D. Lowe
Lieutenant Colonel William H. A. Speer

33rd North Carolina Regiment
Colonel Clark M. Avery
Major Joseph H. Sanders

37th North Carolina Regiment
Colonel William M. Barbour

3rd Brigade
Brigadier General Edward L. Thomas

4th Brigade
Brigadier General Alfred M. Scales
Colonel William Lee J. Lowrance

14th Georgia Regiment
Colonel Robert W. Folsom

13th North Carolina Regiment
Colonel Joseph H. Hyman
Lieutenant Colonel Henry A. Rogers

35th Georgia Regiment
Colonel Bolling H. Holt

16th North Carolina Regiment
Captain Leroy W. Stowe

45th Georgia Regiment
Colonel Thomas J. Simmons

22nd North Carolina Regiment
Lieutenant William L. Mitchell

49th Georgia Regiment
Colonel Samuel T. Player

34th North Carolina Regiment
Colonel William Lee J. Lowrance
Lieutenant Colonel George T. Gordon

38th North Carolina Regiment
Colonel William J. Hoke
Lieutenant Colonel John Ashford
Captain Thornburg

Poague's Artillery Battalion
Major William T. Poague

Abemarle (Virginia) Artillery
Captain James W. Wyatt

Madison (Mississippi) Light Artillery
Captain George Ward

Charlotte (North Carolina) Artillery
Captain Joseph Graham

Warrenton (Virginia) Artillery
Captain James V. Brooke

THIRD CORPS ARTILLERY RESERVE
Colonel R. Lindsey Walker

McIntosh's Battalion
Major David D. McIntosh

Danville (Virginia) Artillery
Captain R. Sidney Rice

Hardaway (Alabama) Artillery
Captain William B. Hurt

2nd Rockbridge (Virginia) Artillery
Lieutenant Samuel Wallace

Richmond (Johnson's) Battery
Captain Marmaduke Johnson

Pegram's Battalion
Major William J. Pegram

Richmond (Crenshaw's) Battery
Lieutenant Andrew B. Johnston

Fredericksburg (Virginia) Artillery
Captain Edward A. Marye

Letcher (Virginia) Artillery
Captain Thomas A. Brander

Pee Dee (South Carolina) Artillery
Lieutenant William E. Zimmerman

Purcell (Virginia) Artillery
Captain Joseph McGraw

Appendix B

NUMBER & LOSSES AT THE BLISS FARM 2-3 JULY 1863

The number of men engaged and casualties suffered during the thirty-two hours of fighting for the Bliss Farm can be estimated based on statistics available in the *Official Records of the Union and Confederate Armies in the War of the Rebellion*, regimental histories, personal narratives, several secondary sources, and by making some good, old-fashioned guesstimates based on both intuitive and deductive reasoning.

Effective Strengths

The prime source used to approximate the number of men engaged was *Regimental Strengths at Gettysburg* by John W. Busey and David G. Martin. Unfortunately, their study does not indicate the number of men per company in the individual regiments. During the fighting for the Bliss Farmstead, in most cases, detachments composed of several companies were sent out to the skirmish lines. To compensate, estimates of company strengths were derived by dividing the total number of men in each regiment by the number of companies present at Gettysburg to approximate the number per company (xx/co). That figure, then, was used to estimate the number of men in the various detachments.

Army of the Potomac

The majority of the Union troops involved at the Bliss Farm were assigned to Brigadier General Alexander Hays' 3rd Division, of the 2nd Army Corps.[1]

1st Brigade
Colonel Samuel S. Carroll

Unit	No. of Companies Present	xx/co	Total
4th Ohio	(6 companies)	@29.9	179
8th Ohio	(10 companies)	-----	209
	Total 1st Brigade (estimated)		388

2nd Brigade
Colonel Thomas A. Smyth

Unit	No. of Companies Present	xx/co	Total
14th Connecticut	(10 companies)	-----	172
1st Delaware	(10 companies)	-----	251
12th New Jersey	(10 companies)	-----	444
108th New York	(2 companies)	@20	40
	Total 2nd Brigade (estimated)		907

3rd Brigade
Colonel George L. Willard

Unit	No. of Companies Present	xx/co	Total
39th New York	(4 companies)	-----	269
111th New York	(2 companies)	@39	78
125th New York	(3 companies)	@39.2	118
126th New York	(4 companies)	@45.5	182
	Total 3rd Brigade (estimated)		647

---

1 John W. Busey and David G. Martin, *Regimental Strengths at Gettysburg*, (Baltimore: Gateway Press, Inc., 1982), pp. 42-44.

Appendix B

Other Units

Unit	No. of Companies Present	xx/co	Total
1st Co. Massachusetts Sharpshooters[2]	(1 company)	-----	42
106th Pennsylvania[3]	(1 company: Co. B)	@28.8	29
2nd Delaware[4]	(10 companies)	-----	150
	Total Other Units (estimated)		221

Thus, the number of Union troops engaged about the Bliss Farm excluding Pickett's Charge were:

Hays' Division
        1st Brigade (Carroll) ------------ 388
        2nd Brigade (Smyth) ------------ 907
        3rd Brigade (Willard) ----------- 647
        Other Units ----------------------- 221
        Grand Total Union Troops ---- 2,163

Army of Northern Virginia

The effective strength of the Confederate forces in the Bliss Farm skirmishes is difficult to estimate. Besides the lack of adequate record-keeping, many logistical records were lost towards the end of the war. Furthermore, there are fewer regimental histories and personal narratives from which to extricate accurate figures.

For example: Though Mahone's Brigade was not actively engaged during the battle, we know men were assigned to picket duty; but Mahone never specified how many companies. Secondly, some units had been engaged prior to the Bliss Farm fight, so we do not know what their effective strengths were on the morning of 2 or 3 July. Therefore, as each brigade was

---

2 Ibid., p. 33. According to Lieutenant Brady, 1st Delaware, some "sharpshooters" were near the farm buildings during the afternoon of July 2nd.

3 Ibid., p. 40.

4 Ibid., p. 38. During 3 July, the remnants of the 2nd Delaware were active on Hays' division skirmish line. According to their official report, the unit lost eighty-four men 2 July. Subtracting this figure from the number engaged, there were approximately 150 men able to fight the following day.

examined and after the *Official Records* and other available sources were consulted, good old-fashioned common sense was used.

In the fight for the Bliss Farm, the majority of the troops involved were part of Major General Richard H. Anderson's Division, and the remainder were from Major General William D. Pender's command.

Anderson's Division

Posey's Brigade[5]
Brigadier General Carnot Posey

Unit	No. of Companies Present	xx/co	Total
12th Mississippi	(10 companies)	-----	305
16th Mississippi	(10 companies)	-----	385
19th Mississippi	(10 companies)	-----	372
48th Mississippi	(10 companies)	-----	256
	Total Posey's Brigade (estimated)		1,318

Mahone's Brigade[6]
Brigadier General William Mahone

Though Mahone's command never left Seminary Ridge en mass during the battle, he did send several detachments out to the picket line. According to D. H. Mahan's *An Elementary Treatise on the Advanced-Guard, Outpost, and Detached Service of Troops and Manner of Posting and Handling Them in Presence of the Enemy,*[7] we know that approximately one-fifth of the main force was to be assigned to the skirmish line to cover a brigade front. Secondly, by examining the casualty returns in the *Official Records* (which are incomplete), one notices that two of Mahone's five regiments (6th and 16th Virginia) suffered fewer losses when compared to his remaining three outfits. Those three each lost approximately the same number of men as the 12th Virginia which listed nineteen casualties.[8] Checking the roster of the

---

5 Ibid., p. 189.

6 Ibid., p. 187.

7 D. H. Mahan, *An Elementary Treatise on the Advanced-Guard, Outpost, and Detached Service of Troops and Manner of Posting and Handling Them in Presence of the Enemy*, New Edition, (New York: John Wiley, 1861, Reprinted Corinth, MS: C. D. Jarnagin, 1985), pp. 83, 84.

8 *The War of the Rebellion: A Compilation of the Official Records of Union and Confederate*

12th Virginia, at least twenty-eight men were casualties. Seventeen of these were probably wounded and captured on the Bliss Farm on 2 July. Upon closer examinations of the 12th's roster, those seventeen men represented seven of the ten companies present, most having been assigned to Companies F, G, and K.[9] Moreover, a perusal of the losses incurred in the 16th regiment suggests that some men may have been present on the skirmish line.[10]

With the above information, what was the most likely scenario for the deployment of Mahone's command? Though all five regiments were held in reserve, some casualties officially reported could be accounted for during the various cannonades during 2-3 July. However, since three regimental commanders reported slightly higher casualties, and the roster of the 16th regiment listed some suspicious losses, those casualties may have been incurred on the skirmish line.

Assuming that each of those five regiments supplied two companies (one-fifth of their total strengths) for picket duty, then a conservative estimate of the number of men from Mahone's Brigade who were engaged in the Bliss Farm fight would be as follows:

Unit	No. of Companies Present	xx/co	Total
12th Virginia	(2 companies)	@34.8	70
16th Virginia	(2 companies)	@38.5	77
41st Virginia	(2 companies)	@27.6	55
61st Virginia	(2 companies)	@35.6	71
Total Mahone's Brigade (estimated)			273

Pender's Division
Scales' (Fourth) Brigade
Colonel William Lee J. Lowrance

According to Lowrance's official report,[11] the brigade had been reduced to about 500 effectives by the morning of 2 July, and one regiment,

---

Armies, 128 volumes, (Washington, D. C.: U. S. War Department, 1880-1901) Vol. 27, pt. 2: p. 343.

9 William D. Henderson, *12th Virginia Infantry*, The Virginia Regimental Series, (Lynchburg, VA: H. E. Howard, Inc., 1984), pp. 106-167.

10 Benjamin H. Trask, 16th Virginia Regiment, The Virginia Regimental Series, (Lynchburg, VA: H. E. Howard, Inc., 1984), pp. 73-128. The regimental roster indicates that at least six men were killed, wounded or captured on 2 July.

11 OR, Vol. 27, pt. 2: p. 671.

the 38th North Carolina, had approximately 116 men able to fight.[12] Thus we can speculate that each of Lowrance's five regiments numbered about 100 men. According to Mahan's *Outpost* manual, normally about ten companies would be detailed for picket duty, but Lowrance reported that he deployed a "strong line of skirmishers."[13] Estimating that Lowrance detached a third of his brigade strength to serve on picket duty, then the approximate number of men in the Bliss Farm fight would be 167.

Lane's (Second) Brigade[14]
Brigadier General James H. Lane

After the first day of battle, Lane's five regiments were positioned between the Fairfield Road and McMillan Woods, suggesting that the majority of his skirmish line probably was situated along Stevens Run north of the Bliss property. Since Scales' command, posted between McMillan and Spangler's Woods, was separated from Lane's Brigade by an artillery battalion (about sixteen cannons), theoretically, Lane's skirmishers had to link up with those from Scales' and consequently were involved in the Bliss Farm fight.

The precise number of men present for duty under Lane is difficult to ascertain. We know that the brigade was partially involved in the final Confederate assault on the Lutheran Seminary on 1 July and participated in Pickett's Charge on the third; but according to the official returns, Lane listed his losses at 660. However, that figure seems rather low considering a figure of 120 has been mentioned for losses incurred on the first day.[15] Subtracting that amount from the effective strength of Lane's command approximated by Martin and Busey, the number present for duty on the morning of 2 July would approximate 1,600.

Since Lane did not mention much concerning the deployment of his picket details in his official report, no individual regiments could be singled out as contributing to those detachments. By assuming that one company per regiment was assigned to picket duty and that a third of Lane's picket

---

12 Walter Clark, ed., *History of the Several Regiments and Battalions from North Carolina in the Great War, 1861-65*, 5 volumes, (Raleigh: E. M. Uzzell, Printer and Bookbinder, 1901), Vol. 1: p. 698.

13 Mahan, *Advanced Guard*, p. 84.

14 Busey and Martin, *Regimental Strengths*, p. 181.

15 Warren W. Hassler, Jr., *Crisis at the Crossroads: The First Day at Gettysburg*, (University, AL: University of Alabama Press, 1970), p. 145.

detail operated in the vicinity of the Bliss Farm, the number of men engaged would approximate 53.

Thomas' (Third) Brigade[16]
Brigadier General Edward L. Thomas

Probably, Thomas supplied some men to the skirmish line during 2 July, but before dusk his brigade was advanced to the Sunken Road, his right flank resting within 300 yards of the Bliss house where his men engaged the skirmishers of the 4th and 8th Ohio along with others from Von Steinwehr's command. Estimating a third of Thomas' Brigade was within rifle range of the Bliss buildings, the number of men engaged would approximate 442.

McGowan's (First) Brigade[17]
Colonel Abner Perrin

Perrin's command was held in reserve north of McMillan Woods for most of 2 July, though some of the South Carolinians were active on the skirmish line engaging the pickets of Von Steinwehr's division. Towards evening, Perrin reinforced his pickets with a full regiment; and later his command joined Thomas' troops when they moved forward to the Sunken Road. The addition of Thomas' and Perrin's skirmishers to the picket line, is corroborated by several Union accounts which mentioned that enemy troops approached their positions from the northwest and from town. Moreover, the account of Blackford Benson of the 1st South Carolina suggests that some part of Perrin's skirmishers were sparring with their counterparts of the 8th Ohio. Guessing that twenty South Carolinians joined with forty additional men from Lane's and/or Thomas' command, then the approximate number of additional troops may have been 60.

Therefore, the estimated total number of Confederate troops involved would be as follows:

Anderson's Division
        Posey's Brigade ---------------- 1,318
        Mahone's Brigade -------------- <u>273</u>
        Total Anderson's Division   1,591

---

16 Busey and Martin, *Regimental Strengths*, p. 179.
17 Ibid.

Pender's Division
    Scales' (Fourth) Brigade -------------------- 167
    Lane's (Second) Brigade -------------------- 53
    Thomas' (Third) Brigade ------------------ 442
    McGowan's (First) Brigade
      (Including displaced skirmishers
      from Lane and Thomas' commands) --- <u>60</u>
    Total Pender's Division   722

Grand Total Confederate Troops (estimated)   2,313

Casualty Figures

An approximation of the casualties suffered by both armies in the quagmire of the Bliss Farm can be estimated by analyzing the *Official Records*, personal narratives, and regimental histories.

Army of the Potomac

Hays' 3rd Division
Carroll's 1st Brigade

4th Ohio Regiment[18] ----------------- 26
8th Ohio Regiment[19] ---------------- <u>52</u>
    Total 1st Brigade   78

---

18 According to the *Official Records*, the total number of casualties for the 4th Ohio was 31, and those of Companies G and I numbered approximately 21. Assuming the losses suffered during the East Cemetery Hill fight was 5, then the total casualties suffered on the skirmish line along the Emmitsburg Road would be 26.

19 *Letter from Franklin Sawyer to John B. Bachelder*, dated 24 May 1886, John B. Bachelder Papers, New Hampshire Historical Society, on microfilm, Gettysburg National Military Park Library.

Smyth's 2nd Brigade

14th Connecticut[20] ------------------	34
1st Delaware[21] -----------------------	58
12th New Jersey[22] --------------------	71
108th New York[23] --------------------	10
Casualties 2nd Brigade	173

Willard's 3rd Brigade

39th New York[24] -----------------------	26
111th New York[25] --------------------	10
125th New York[25] --------------------	15
126th New York[25] --------------------	20
Casualties 3rd Brigade	71

---

20 Total casualties for the 14th Connecticut over the three days were 66. In Busey and Martin, the total number engaged approximated 172, thus about 106 men were present after Pickett's Charge. Thus, the number lost on the skirmish line was approximately 34.

21 OR, Vol. 27, pt. 1: p. 469; and *John L. Brady to Bachelder*, dated 25 May 1886, p. 14.

22 Frederick A. Jago, *12th New Jersey Volunteers: 1862-65*, (Haddenfield, N. J.: Elmer Garfield Van Name, 1967), p. 9.

23 George Washburn, *A Complete History and Record of the 108th Regiment New York Volunteers: From 1862-1894 Together with Roster, Letters, Rebel Oaths of Allegiance, Rebel Passes, Reminiscences, Like Sketches, Photographs, etc.*, (Rochester, NY: E. R. Andrews, 1894), p. 49. Two companies had been assigned to the skirmish line on 3 July, but no references were made to any losses suffered along the Emmitsburg Road during the entire battle. Though the possibility does exist that no one assigned to the picket detail was injured significantly enough to necessitate a visit to the surgeon and be recorded as a casualty, this seems highly unlikely. However, the 39th New York Regiment had suffered some 26 casualties on the picket line during 2 July, or approximately 5 casualties per company. Using this ratio, the 108th New York possibly suffered ten casualties on the skirmish line.

24 OR, Vol. 27, pt. 1: p. 472. See report of Lieutenant Colonel James M. Bull, 126th New York.

25 No specific figures available. Using the ratio of 5 men/company derived for the losses of the 39th New York, the number would approximate the one given.

Other Units

106th Pennsylvania (Co. B)[26] ---------- 17
1st Company Massachusetts S. S.[27] ---- 8
2nd Delaware[28] -------------------------- 10
    Casualties Other Units   35

Thus, the estimated casualty figures for the Union forces involved in the struggle for the Bliss Farm, excluding Pickett's Charge, would be as follows:

Hays' Division
    1st Brigade ----------------------------- 78
    2nd Brigade ---------------------------- 173
    3rd Brigade ---------------------------- 71
Other Units ---------------------------------- 35
    Total Union Casualties (estimated) 357

Army of Northern Virginia

Confederate casualty figures are the most difficult to estimate, for many of the returns listed in the *Official Records* are highly suspect. For example: Posey's Brigade officially suffered eighty-three casualties – killed and wounded – but no missing were listed. However, numerous accounts from the 12th New Jersey indicated that ninety-two Confederates were captured at the Bliss barn; and those accounts implied that most were members of the 16th Mississippi. Indeed, according to an entry in *Grandfather's Journal*,[29] seventeen men from Posey's Brigade were captured over three days, and seven were from the 16th. Secondly, in his official report, Mahone states that thirty-nine of his men were captured although they are not listed in the *Official Records*. Moreover, the brigades of Pender's Division had been engaged on all three days of the battle, suffering most on the first and third; but the casualty figures for the three days were

---

26 Ward, *History 106th Pennsylvania*, p. 191. An estimated 5 casualties were added for the second assault on the Bliss barn 2 July.

27 OR, Vol. 27, pt. 1: p. 176.

28 No figures available. This is a guesstimate.

29 Austin C. Dobbins, *Grandfather's Journal: Co. B, 16th Mississippi Infantry, Harris' Brigade, Mahone's Division, Hill's Corps, Army of Northern Virginia, May 22, 1861 - July 15, 1865*, (Dayton: Morningside House, Inc., 1988), p. 150.

not itemized per day. In the final analysis, any figures are, for the most part, speculative at best.

R. H. Anderson's Division

Posey's Brigade
    In the official returns, Posey's command is listed as losing eighty-three men with at least seventeen captured.[30] Guesstimating that actually about two-thirds of the soldiers captured at the Bliss barn were Mississippians, that would increase Posey's casualties by approximately 45 men. Therefore, the total estimated casualties would be 145.

Mahone's Brigade
    In his official report, Mahone listed his losses at 102 during the three days.[31] Guessing that twenty men may have been injured and/or killed during the cannonade of 3 July, Mahone's casualties for the Bliss Farm skirmishes would approximate 82.
    The estimated total casualties for Anderson's Division would be:

    R. H. Anderson's Division
            Posey's Brigade ------------- 145
            Mahone's Brigade ----------- <u>82</u>
            Total   227

Pender's Division

Scales' Brigade
    Any estimate of casualties inflicted on this command in the Bliss Farm fight would be pure conjecture. We know that most of the losses were incurred during 1 and 3 July, but some men surely fell during the skirmishing around the Bliss Farm, probably during the attack and repulse of the 1st Delaware during the morning of 2 July. Since the casualties of the 1st Delaware were reported as being thirty-two during the day,[32] and estimating that three-fourths of those were incurred in the morning, we speculate that Scales' pickets suffered one and a half times that amount or approximately 36.

---

30 OR, Vol. 27, pt. 2: p. 343; and Dobbins, *Grandfather's Journal*, p. 150.
31 Ibid., p. 621.
32 OR, Vol. 27, pt. 1: pp. 468 & 469.

Lane's Brigade
Like Scales' command, men from Lane's Brigade had been on the skirmish line since the early morning hours of 2 July, but we do not know how long they remained on picket duty. Since there is no documentation that indicates the contrary, we assume that Lane's men were present for the better part of the day or about twice as long as those from Scales' Brigade. Estimating that Lane's losses were double those of Scales' skirmish details, an approximation of Lane's casualties would be 72.

Thomas' Brigade
Though some of Thomas' Georgians surely had been assigned to the skirmish line during 2 July, around 7:00 PM the bulk of the brigade was advanced to the Sunken Road within 300 yards of the Bliss house. Assuming that half of Thomas's casualties were incurred near the Bliss Farm,[33] an estimate of his losses would be 138.

Compiling these estimates into table form:

Grand Total Confederate Casualties

Total R. H. Anderson's Division	227
Pender's Division	
Scales' Brigade	36
Lane's Brigade	72
Thomas' Brigade	138
Total Confederate Casualties (estimated)	473

Therefore, rounding the estimates to the nearest ten, and calculating the percentage loss of the effective strength of the total number of men engaged we have the following:

Estimate Numbers and Losses
Bliss Farm Skirmishes Excluding Pickett's Charge

	Effective Strength	Losses	% Loss
Union	2,160	360	17%
Confederate	2,310	470	20%
Grand Total	4,470	830	19%

---

33 Thomas' Brigade War Department Plaque, Gettysburg Battlefield, located on West Confederate Avenue at McMillan Woods.

Appendix C[1]

UNION SOLDIERS KILLED OR MORTALLY WOUNDED ON THE BLISS FARM[2] BURIED AT THE EVERGREEN AND GETTYSBURG NATIONAL CEMETERIES

Name and Rank	Unit	Location of Grave	When and Where Killed or Mortally Wounded[3]
1. Adams, George W. (Pvt)	Co. F (NJ) 12 NJ A-14		KIA (7/3/63) East of Bliss Farm
2. Bain (Baird), William (Pvt)	Co. G (OH) 4 OH D-15		KIA (7/2/63) E. Trostle's
3. Barkley, John K. (Sgt)	Co. C (OH) 8 OH A-20		KIA (7/2/63) Near Bliss Farm
4. Clement, Moses G. (Pvt)	Co. G (CT) 14 CT A-04		KIA (7/3/63) Bliss Barn
5. Collins, David W. (Pvt)	Co. G (OH) 4 OH D-14		KIA (7/2/63) E. Trostle's
6. Davis, Asa O. (Pvt)	Co. G (OH) 4 OH E-13		KIA (7/2/63) E. Trostle's

1 Edmund J. Raus, Jr. ed, *Union Civil War Veterans Buried at Gettysburg*, 1977. Transcript on file Gettysburg National Military Park Library.

2 Excludes those men killed or mortally wounded during Pickett's Charge.

3 KIA = Killed in Action; and MW = Mortally Wounded.

7. Dorsey, William	Co. D	(DE)	KIA (7/3/63)
(Pvt)	1 DE	A-03	Bliss Farm
8. Edgar, Addison E.	Co. G	(OH)	MW (7/2/63)
(2nd Lt)	4 OH	D-16	E. Trostle's
9. Kipka, John C.	Co. A	Evergreen	MW (7/3/63)
(Sgt)	8 OH		Near Bliss Farm
10. Martin, George H.	Co. G	(OH)	KIA (7/2/63)
(Pvt)	4 OH	B-21	E. Trostle's
11. Myers, Andrew	Co. G	(OH)	KIA (7/2/63)
(Pvt)	4 OH	D-17	E. Trostle's
12. Sheets, John B.	Co. D	(DE)	KIA (7/3/63)
(Cpl)	1 DE	A-04	Bliss Farm
13. Shaub, Samuel J.	Co. I	Evergreen	KIA (7/2/63)
(2nd Lt)	4 OH		E. Trostle's
14. Smith, William H.	Co. B	(PA)	KIA (7/2/63)
(2nd Lt)	106 PA	C-42	Near Bliss Barn
15. Stark, Henry C.	Co. I	(OH)	KIA (7/2/63)
(Pvt)	4 OH	B-17	E. Trostle's
16. Tracy, Philip F.	Co. G	(OH)	KIA (7/2 - 7/3/63)
(Sgt)	8 OH	B-22	Near Bliss Barn
17. Wagner, Adolphus	Co. C	(NY)	MW (7/2/63)
(2nd Lt)	39 NY	E-54	Bliss Farm

Appendix D

CONFEDERATES KILLED OR MORTALLY WOUNDED POSSIBLY IN CONNECTION WITH THE BLISS FARM ACTIONS*

Name	Unit	Command
1. Bankston, T.	Co. C, 16 Miss.	Posey's Brigade
2. Campbell, F. R. M.	Adjutant, 48 Miss.	Posey's Brigade
3. Coleman, B.	Co. A, 19 Miss.	Posey's Brigade
4. Georgehegan (sic?), T. L.	Co. F, 19 Miss.	Posey's Brigade
5. Johnson, H. C.	Co. F, 19 Miss.	Posey's Brigade
6. Wright, T. I.	Co. B, 16 Va.	Mahone's Brigade

---

* John W. C. O'Neal, *Record of Confederate Burials: Journal of Doctor John W. C. O'Neal, M. D.*, Transcript on file Gettysburg National Park Library.

Appendix E

PARTIAL CASUALTY LIST
12th & 16th Virginia Regiments, Mahone's Brigade[1]

Men Killed, Wounded or Captured Possibly During the Bliss Farm Fighting 2 July 1863.

Name and Rank	Regiment, Company	Remarks[2]
1. Barrett, George H. (Pvt)	16th, F	WIA
2. Bennett, John (Pvt)	12th, G	WIA & POW
3. Cordle, Richard H. (Pvt)	12th, F	DOW
4. Eason, Dempsey (Pvt)	12th, F	POW
5. Gray, Joseph (Pvt)	12th, F	POW
6. Jones, Samuel G. (Sgt)	12th, F	WIA
7. McGlemore, John W. (Pvt)	12th, K	MWIA & POW
8. Mendez, Samuel P. (Pvt)	12th, F	WIA & POW
9. Mitchell, William R. (Sgt)	12th, F	WIA
10. Nunnally, Edward J. (Pvt)	12th, H	KIA
11. Pagand, Thaddeus (Sgt)	12th, E	WIA & POW
12. Richardson, James H. (Sgt)	16th, C	WIA
13. Rodgers, Philip (2nd Cpl)	16th, B	MWIA & POW
14. Scoggin, John J. (Cpl)	12th, F	POW
15. Sledge, Asa M. (Pvt)	12th, F	POW
16. Smith, Walthall W. (Pvt)	12th, K	WIA
17. Sykes, William H. T. (Pvt)	12th, A	MWIA
18. Weeks, Walter W. (Pvt)	12th, K	POW

1 William D. Henderson, *12th Virginia Infantry*, The Virginia Regimental Series, (Lynchburg, VA: H. E. Howard, Inc., 1984), pp. 106-167; and Benjamin H. Trask, *16th Virginia Infantry*, The Virginia Regimental Series, (Lynchburg, VA: H. E. Howard, Inc., 1986), pp. 73-128.

2 DOW = Died of Wounds; KIA = Killed in Action; MWIA = Mortally Wounded in Action; POW = Prisoner of War; and WIA = Wounded in Action.

19.	Wells, Winfield (Pvt)	12th, K	WIA
20.	Wills, Ocellus (Pvt)	12th, A	WIA & POW
21.	Wineborne, Elisha J. (Pvt)	16th, A	WIA
22.	Woodhouse, John T. (Maj)	16th, F & S	WIA
23.	Wright, Thomas J. (4th Cpl)	16th, B	KIA

Appendix F

THE LIFE AND TIMES OF WILLIAM BLISS

William Bliss, the youngest surviving child of twelve siblings, was born on 4 September 1799 in the village of Rehoboth, Bristol County, Massachusetts. This village is located approximately twenty miles east of Providence, Rhode Island. His father Dr. James Bliss, also born and raised in Rehoboth, and one of its leading citizens, had apprenticed under Doctors Brownson and Blackinton before initiating his medical practice at Wrentham circa 1778 at the age of twenty-two. While Dr. Bliss tended to the needs of the community, he met and later married Hannah Guild of Attleborough. He purchased the old Timothy Redaway farmstead at Rehoboth about a year later on 28 June 1779, and converted the farmhouse into an inn. During the American Revolution, in 1780, Dr. Bliss served as a surgeon's mate in Colonel Thomas Carpenter's regiment of infantry.[1]

After the Revolution, Dr. Bliss became one of the more respected citizens of the village of Rehoboth. Serving as the clerk for the trustees of

---

[1] James N. Arnold, *Vital Records of Rehoboth, 1642-1896: Marriages, Intentions, Births, Deaths With Supplements Containing the Record of 1896, Colonial Returns, Lists of the Early Settlers, Purchases, Freeman Inhabitants, the Soldiers Serving in Phillip's War and the Revolution*, (Providence, RI: Narragansett Historical Publications Co, 1897), p. 539; Leonard Bliss, Jr, *History of Rehoboth, Bristol County, Massachusetts: Comprising a History of the Present Towns of Rehoboth, Seekonk, and Pawtacket From Their Settlement to the Present Time; Together With Sketches of Attleborough, Cumberland and Part of Swansey and Barrington to the Time that They Separated from the Original Town*, (Boston: Otis, Broaders and Co, 1836), p. 274; and Richard LeBaron Bowen, *Early Rehoboth: Documented Historical Studies of Families and Events in Plymouth Township*, 4 volumes (Concord, Mass: Rumford Press, 1945), 1: p. 48f, 2: p. 122, 4: pp. 21, 24, 32, and 145.

the First Congregational Society for many years, he also was elected as Rehoboth's representative to the General Court of Massachusetts in 1815, 1816, and 1820. As the last remaining years of his life passed, James had acquired additional tracts of land, which enlarged his estate. Leonard Bliss, Jr. wrote that his grandfather, James, "was a man of sound judgment, strict integrity, and great industry and economy."[2] Into this busy and prosperous atmosphere William was born and spent his first twenty-six years.

For William, life must have been hectic growing up on a working farm and tavern with three brothers and seven sisters. Possibly travelers that stayed at the Bliss' inn filled the boy's head with tales of distant lands, and those stories probably supplemented the education that the good doctor made sure his children received. But tragedy struck on 5 October 1816 when his mother passed away at the age of fifty-two. Dr. Bliss, who probably was ill-equipped to raise eleven children, run the farm and tavern, and practice his medical profession, married Sarah (Sally) Deane of neighboring Dighton a short time later.[3]

The grief and sorrow that William must have felt after the loss of his mother slowly disappeared, and seven years later Cupid's arrow struck when he met and fell in love with Adeline Carpenter, a relative of his father's former regimental commander. On 1 February 1823 the young couple registered their intentions and a month later on 13 March, Adeline's twenty-third birthday, they were united in holy matrimony by the Reverend Otis Thompson at Rehoboth. Nine months later, the newlyweds were blessed with their first child, Amanda Malvina, born 8 January 1824, followed eight months later by their second daughter, Sarah Gooding Bliss.[4]

By 1826, with the increasing population and possibly due to inflated costs of real estate around his hometown, William searched for greener and wider pastures. Possibly hearing of virgin farm areas in northeastern Pennsylvania from land speculators or bankers in nearby Providence, he decided to move his family to a "Division allotted to William Russell by the Marshall of Western District or Territory," today known in part as Warren Township, Bradford County. At this location their third daughter, Adeline Elizabeth, was born on 30 March 1828.[5] Nine months later, on 17

---

2 Rev. George F. Tilton, A. M, *A History of Rehoboth, Massachusetts: Its History For 215 Years, 1643-1918 in Which is Incorporated the Vital Parts of the Original History of the Town, Published in 1836, and Written By Leonard Bliss, Jr,* (Boston: Louis E. Crosscup Co, 1918), pp. 322 and 323; and Bliss, *History of Rehoboth,* pp. 169 and 274.

3 Bliss, *History of Rehoboth,* p. 274.

4 Arnold, *Vital Records,* pp. 37 and 543. Also see section on Intentions.

5 Bristol County Court House, Probate Registry, Taunton, MA: Books 74: pp. 434 and 479

December, William officially purchased a seventy-seven acre farm about a mile southwest of the village of Warren Center within the "Rhode Island Tract." James William, their first son, was born on 12 May 1830.[6]

Apparently during the winter of 1830-1831, Bliss decided to continue his migration westward with his wife and four children. On 20 April 1831 he officially sold his farm in Warren Township, and within two years the family settled in the Town[7] of Gerry (pronounced Geary) located about ten miles north of Jamestown, Chautauqua County, New York. Their fourth daughter, Frances Amelia, was born there on 8 June 1833.[8] With a fresh outlook and new scenery, the Bliss family started their life anew amongst the long, rolling hills of southwestern New York.

Unfortunately, the mid-1830's were tragic for William and Adeline. On 29 September 1834, William's father died at the ripe old age of seventy-seven years, and to claim his share of the estate, documentation suggests that William returned to Massachusetts, apparently leaving Adeline and the children in upstate New York. After the distribution of the James Bliss estate, William's inheritance was assessed at just over $3,000 of the total legacy valued at $25,369.07. Before leaving Rehoboth, William sold a portion of his inheritance (several pieces of real estate) but retained his interests in a sawmill and some pasture land.[9] Shortly after his return to Chautauqua County and probably using some of his inheritance, William purchased a ninety-five acre farm situated about a mile east-southeast of Sinclairsville, located in the northern section of the Town of Gerry on 1

---

and 75: p. 343; and 3rd U. S. Census, 1830, Warren Township, Bradford County, Pennsylvania.

6 Bradford County Court House, Towanda, Pennsylvania, Office of the Register and Recorder, Deed Records, Deed Book 8: p. 178; *Map of the Providence, Rhode Island Tract, circa 1830*, Copy in possession of Jeffrey W. Geiss, Land Surveyor, George K. Jones Associates, 1 Popular Street, Towanda, Pa; and *William Bliss Family Memorial*, Evergreen Cemetery, Sinclairsville, Town of Charlotte, Chautauqua County, New York.

7 In New England and upstate New York, "Towns" are equivalent to townships. For example: in Chautauqua County, the Bliss Farm, located in Town of Gerry, was situated near the village of Sinclairsville situated in the Town of Charlotte.

8 Chautauqua County Court House, Mayville, New York, Deed Records, Book 16: p. 428; *Bliss Memorial*; and Bradford County (PA), Deed Book 9: p. 325.

9 *Headstone of Dr. James Bliss*, Village Cemetery, Rehoboth, Bristol County, Massachusetts. See also Arnold, *Vital Records*; Bristol County, Deed Book 146: pp. 413 and 485. In the deed found on page 413, it infers that William Bliss was present in Massachusetts during 1835; and Bristol County, Probate Book 74: pp. 434 and 479 and 75: p. 343.

October 1835. There, William Bliss and family resided for the next twenty years.[10]

But death stalked the Bliss household. Five-year old James died on 18 June 1835, followed two years later by a second son who died on 12 March 1837 at the age of seventeen days. Both deaths were possibly a result of the bitterly cold winters of 1836 and 1837. Then, on 14 June 1846, their eldest daughter, Amanda passed away. Yet despite these personal tragedies, Adeline, William, and the surviving children remained in Chautauqua County working their farm. William also served as Supervisor of the Town of Gerry for two terms – 1839 and 1849.[11]

By the 1850's, life in upstate New York was no longer appealing to Bliss and his family, and according to daughter Frances, they decided to move to a warmer climate. After selling his farm on 2 July 1856,[12] and after the marriage of daughter Adeline to a Daniel B. Harris of Union City, Erie County, Pennsylvania on that 21 October,[13] Bliss moved his family to the bustling market town of Gettysburg. On 7 April 1857 William and Adeline purchased from Alexander Cobean, for the sum of $1,960.96, a fifty-three acre tract complete with house, barn, and orchard. A year later, William acquired an additional seven acres adjacent to his new farm from John Cunningham, a former associate of Mr. Cobean.[14] Two years later their daughter, Adeline Harris, made an extended visit, and on 11 January 1860, Bliss's second grandchild, Esther Isabel Harris, was born[15] on the farm. Thus, at the age of fifty-nine and with an initial capital investment of slightly over $2,100, William, his wife Adeline, and daughters Frances and Sarah had started life anew in Pennsylvania. However, Bliss had no way of knowing that three years later the grand course of human events would leave his family practically destitute.

---

10 Chautauqua County, Deed Book 16: p. 428.

11 John P. Downs and Fenwick Y. Hedley, eds., *History of Chautauqua County, New York and Its People*, (Boston: American Historical Society, Inc., 1921), 2 Volumes, 1: p. 51; and Andrew W. Young, *History of Chautauqua County, New York: From Its First Settlement to the Present Time*, (Buffalo: Matthews and Warrren, 1875), p. 400; *Bliss Memorial*. Date of Amanda's passing appears on her headstone.

12 Note of Frances A. Bliss, unsigned and undated, transcript in possession of Mrs. Marilyn Hershberger, R. D. #4, Union City, PA 16438; and Chautauqua County, Deed Book 82: p. 477.

13 Aaron Bliss, *Bliss Family in America*, I: p. 494.

14 Adams County Court House, Gettysburg, Pennsylvania, Office of the Register and Recorder, Deed Books: U: p. 80 (52.99 acres) and U: p. 218 (7.30 acres).

15 Aaron Bliss, *Bliss Family in America*, I: p. 494.

Of all the farmers that had been affected by General Robert E. Lee's Gettysburg Campaign, many returned to find most, if not all, of their crops and livestock gone. However, their homes were intact though slightly worse for the wear. The Bliss family, however, amidst the scenes of death, destruction, and a nation's agony, discovered that only the land remained – all else was gone.

At the age of sixty-three, then, William Bliss and his family had to start life anew. Within three weeks after the battle, by that 29 July, Mr. Bliss had compiled an inventory of "his property destroyed in his house and Barn when burned by the Union Army in order to dislodge rebel sharpshooters." He estimated the cost of lost personal property to be $1,256.08.[16] As the months formed a year, apparently William had to have the signature of the Justice of the Peace on his inventory authenticated. On 6 December 1864, he appeared before Jacob Bushy, Prothonotary of the Court of Common Pleas of Adams County for that purpose.[17]

As the wheels of governmental red tape turned ever so slowly, the Bliss family continued to reside in the Gettysburg vicinity, and by the end of the war, William could not wait any longer. Though he tried to sell the remnants of his farm for $3,000, there were no takers. Finally, on 9 October 1865, William sold it to his neighbor, Nicholas Codori, for $1,000.[18] Accounting for their initial capital investment of $2,143.46 and their loss of personal property, the Bliss family had to absorb a capital loss of almost $2,400.

About the time they sold their farm near Gettysburg, William decided to return to Chautauqua County. After settling in the Town of Busti, he purchased a seventy-eight acre farm in the northern section of the Town of Kiantone, several miles south of Jamestown on 27 November 1865.[19] Two years after they settled into their new home, William compiled an Abstract of Application for Damages under an Act, dated April 9, 1868:

> designed to help in the relief of the citizens of those
> counties in central part of the state whose property was

---

16 Commonwealth of Pennsylvania, Department of the Auditor-General, Damage Claims under the Acts of April 23, 1863, April 9, 1869, and May 27, 1871, Adams County, William Bliss. See Inventory.

17 Ibid.

18 Ibid. See affidavits filed by Nicholas Codori, and David Kendlehart and David McCreary, dated January 1864; and Adams County, Deed Book 61: p. 603.

19 Chautauqua County, Deed Book 118: p. 40.

destroyed, damaged, or appropriated for public use, and in common defense, in the war to suppress the Rebellion.[20]

In this abstract, William tallied the fair market value of his farm and personal items lost during the Battle at Gettysburg and the maximum amount of damages he would claim was $3,256.08. On 28 December 1868, Mr. Bliss was in the Chautauqua County Clerk's Office having another damage claim notarized,[21] but before it was accepted, apparently two additional affidavits were required, those of Nicholas Codori and the other from David Kendlehart and David McCreary.[22]

For a second time, the Bliss family patiently waited for the resolution of their damage claims, but tragedy struck the Bliss household when Sarah died in 1869.[23] However, on 27 September 1871, for a fourth time during an eight-year period, Bliss submitted his claims attesting "that he has never sold or assigned his claim, that he never received any compensation for his property from any source, and that no portion of it was ever retained by him."[24] Two months later, a glimmer of hope appeared on the horizon, for Bliss received notification that on 3 November the Commonwealth of Pennsylvania would award to William Bliss $3,216.48 for his losses sustained during the Battle at Gettysburg. The award was granted under another act, approved by the Pennsylvania legislature on 27 May 1871, entitled "An act to authorize the liquidation of damages sustained by the citizens of Pennsylvania during the late Rebellion."[25]

This glimmer of hope, however, was doused by the waters of indecision, buck-passing, and compromise between Federal and state agencies involved. Apparently, the Commonwealth of Pennsylvania never paid the awarded amount, and eight more years passed with no apparent resolution forthcoming, and by the close of 1879, the damage claims of William Bliss were submitted to the Federal Committee of War Claims of the House of Representatives. Again, William stated his claim for $3,256.08 of restitution, but a year later, in a letter from the Quartermaster-General of the Army, the claim was:

> returned to the Auditor-General of the State of Pennsylvania... as it appeared that the claim was one

---

20 Bliss, *Damage Claims*, See Abstract of Application.

21 Ibid.

22 Ibid. See affidavits from Codori, and Kendlehart and McCreary.

23 *Bliss Memorial*.

24 Bliss, *Damage Claims*.

25 Ibid.

against the state and not property received or taken for use
of and used by the U. S. Army.[26]

Probably this argument over which agency had jurisdiction continued
for another eight years, for numerous letters passed between the Secretary
of War and several War Claims Committee members, one as late as
February 1888.[27]

However, Father Time caught up with William and Adeline Bliss
before the restitution issue was settled. On 18 August 1888, after "88 years,
11 months, and 15 days" William passed away on his farm near Jamestown,
and on Independence Day 1889, Adeline followed her husband of sixty-five
years in death.[28]

Nonetheless, at the age of fifty-five, Frances A. Bliss, the youngest and
sole-surviving child, continued to push for some sort of restitution. After
the death of her parents, Frances attempted to run the family farm, but it
became too much of a chore, for she sold the farmstead in exchange for cash
and property on the south side of Jamestown. Unfortunately, the
purchasers of the farm did not inform Frances that they were in arrears with
their mortgage payments on her new house and lot. On 11 August 1897,
after Frances could not keep up with those mortgage obligations,
foreclosure proceedings (Lis Pendens) were initiated.[29]

At the age of sixty-four years, Frances was in dire financial straits and
needed some assistance, but shortly thereafter she must have found a
sympathetic ear in the United States Senate, which resulted in Bill #6303,
designed in part to pay the damage claims to the descendants of William
Bliss. However, President Theodore Roosevelt and the U. S. Supreme
Court sounded a death knell for the Bill and any further damage claims. In
a letter, dated 18 December 1902, from the Quartermaster-General's Office
addressed to the Secretary of War, the following was written:

> So far as this bill would authorize the payment for damages
> to property in necessary military operations [the burning of
> the Bliss buildings to eliminate the threat of Confederate
> sharpshooters]..., attention is invited to the Supreme Court
> decision in the case... United States v. Pacific Railroad (120
> U. S. 227).... [The] Supreme Court said:

---

26 Ibid. Abstract for Award, dated May 22, 1871.

27 Ibid. See correspondences between the Quartermaster-Master, U. S. Army and the
  Secretary of War, dated 9, 14, and 17 February 1888.

28 Fenton Historical Center, Jamestown, New York, *Card Catalogue of Marriages and Deaths*.

29 Chautauqua County, Lis Pendens Files, File #A-390, Envelope #2633, Case #26,627.

That the principle that for any injuries to
a destruction of private property in neces-
sary military operations...the government
is not responsible is thus considered established. Compensation has been made
in several cases, it is true, but it has
generally been stated by the President in
his veto message (a matter of bounty
rather than strict legal right).[30]

In essence, the Court ruled that the Federal Government was not
responsible for the destruction of private property during actual combat
situations, but implies that if Union soldiers would have disassembled the
house and barn and used the materials to build fortifications; if the food and
farm implements, cattle, livestock, or personal belongings of the Bliss family
would have been used by the Federal forces, then Bliss and his descendants
would have had a valid claim for damages. Unfortunately, the burning of
the house and barn and the subsequent loss of personal property was one of
the many misfortunes of war.

Though the veto of Senate Bill #6303 must have been a severe
financial blow to Frances, apparently she persevered and raised the funds to
pay the mortgage, for she retained title to her home in Jamestown until she
lost some of her faculties. According to the text of a deed dated 16 August
1920 for the sale of her Jamestown property, Frances was described as "an
incompetent person" residing at a Union City, Erie County, Pennsylvania
medical facility near the Harris family farm. She passed away in 1921 and
was buried in the Evergreen Cemetery in Sinclairsville next to her parents
and four siblings.[31]

---

30 Bliss, *Damage Claims*.
31 Ibid. Chautauqua County Deed Book 463: pp. 442 and 443; and *Bliss Memorial*.

PHOTOGRAPHS
AND
ILLUSTRATIONS

Lieutenant General Ambrose P. Hill

Commanded Third Corps, Army of Northern Virginia. On
2 July, Hill's hands-off approach to command contributed to the
breakdown of the en echelon attacks on Cemetery Ridge.
Credit: MOLLUS Collection at USAMHI

Major General Richard H. Anderson

Commanded a division, Hill's Corps. Without the
direction from corps command, Anderson attempted to
rectify the situation that had developed at the Bliss
Farm.

Credit: MOLLUS Collection at USAMHI

Brigadier General Carnot Posey

Commanded a brigade, Anderson's Division. On 2 July, most of Posey's Mississippi troops were committed to the fight for the Bliss Farm before the en echelon mode of assaults reached his sector of the Confederate line.
Credit: Leib Image Archives

1st Lieutenant James R. Bell

Member Co. B, 12th Mississippi Regiment, Posey's
Brigade. Present at Gettysburg.
Credit: *Confederate Veteran* Magazine

Private Franklin Lafayette Riley

Member Co. C, 16th Mississippi Regiment, Posey's Brigade.
Present at Gettysburg.
Credit: *Confederate Veteran* Magazine

Colonel Nathaniel H. Harris

Commanded 19th Mississippi Regiment, Posey's Brigade. Harris' regiment and the 48th Mississippi, the right wing of Posey's Brigade, along with Wright's Georgians, advanced east of the Emmitsburg Road to within sixty yards of Brown's Battery B, 1st Rhode Island Light Artillery, that was positioned about 100 yards southwest of the "copse of trees."

Credit: MOLLUS Collection at USAMHI

129

Brigadier General William "Scrappy Billy" Mahone

Commanded a brigade, Anderson's Division. His brigade was not
heavily involved in the battle, delegated instead to support
Confederate artillery on Seminary Ridge.
Credit: MOLLUS Collection at USAMHI

Brigadier General William D. Pender

Commanded a division, Hill's Corps. At a critical moment, Pender
received his mortal wound on 2 July near the southeast corner of
McMillan Woods, possibly as he was investigating the stymied
situation at the Bliss Farm.
Credit: MOLLUS Collection at USAMHI

Colonel Abner Perrin

Commanded McGowan's Brigade, Pender's
Division. His and Thomas' brigades failed to
advance past the "Sunken Road" due in part to the
positioning of the 8th Ohio on the broad, flat knoll
as a result of the Bliss Farm actions.
Credit: MOLLUS Collection at
USAMHI

Major General Winfield S. Hancock

Commanded 2nd Corps, Army of the Potomac.
Credit: MOLLUS Collection at USAMHI

Brigadier General Alexander Hays

Commanded 3rd Division, 2nd Corps.
Credit: MOLLUS Collection at USAMHI

Colonel Samuel S. Carroll

Commanded 1st Brigade, 3rd Division. Though most of
his brigade was sent to reinforce the Union troops on
East Cemetery Hill during the evening of 2 July, the
majority of his Ohio troops fought near the Bliss Farm.
Credit: MOLLUS Collection at USAMHI

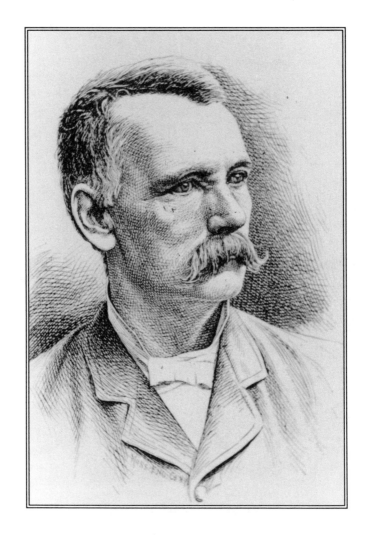

Lieutenant Colonel Leonard W. Carpenter

Commanded 4th Ohio Volunteers, 1st Brigade, 3rd Division, 2nd Corps. Six companies of his command served on the skirmish line near the Bliss Farm on 2 July; Cos. G and I remaining near the Emanuel Trostle residence until 11 PM.

Credit Washburn's *History of the 108th New York*

Lieutenant Colonel Franklin Sawyer

Commanded 8th Ohio Volunteers, 1st Brigade, 3rd Division, 2nd Corps. Ordered out to support Cos. G and I, 4th Ohio on 2 July, Sawyer's men stymied the Confederate assaults at the Bliss Farm. The following day, the 8th Ohio found itself strategically placed to enfilade the right of Pettigrew and Trimble's commands.
Credit: MOLLUS Collection at USAMHI

Colonel Thomas A. Smyth

Commanded 2nd Brigade, 3rd Division, 2nd Corps. Most of the
Union units engaged at the Bliss Farm were from his command.
Credit: MOLLUS Collection at USAMHI

Captain Theron E. Parsons

A member of the 108th New York Volunteers who served as an
aide-de-camp to Colonel Smyth.
Credit: Washburn's *History of the 108th New York*

J. PARKE POSTLES,
Captain, Co. A, 1st Del. Infantry.
Highest rank attained: Inspector-Gen'l,
U. S. V.
Born in Camden, Del., Sept. 28, 1840.

Captain James Parke Postles

A member of the 1st Delaware Volunteers who served as
an aide-de-camp to Colonel Smyth. Postles was awarded
the Congressional Medal of Honor for his ride out to the
Bliss Farm on 3 July.
Credit: Beyer & Keydel, *Deeds of Valor*

Captain John L. Sparks

Commanded Co. K, 1st Delaware Volunteers. Wounded 2 July on the Bliss Farm, Sparks' company was positioned to the right of the Philadelphia Brigade's advanced picket line.
Credit: Roger D. Hunt Collection at USAMHI

Captain Henry F. Chew

Commanded Co. I, 12th New Jersey Volunteers. Served on picket
duty during the late morning and afternoon 2 July.
Credit: NJ State Library, Bureau of Archives &
History

Captain Samuel B. Jobes

Co. G, 12th New Jersey Volunteers. Commanded the detachment of Jerseymen who charged the Bliss barn on 2 July, capturing about 92 prisoners.

Credit: NJ State Library, Bureau of Archives & History

Captain Richard S. Thompson

Co. K, 12th New Jersey Volunteers.   Commanded the
detachment of Jerseyians that charged the Bliss barn on 3 July,
capturing about three prisoners.

Credit: NJ State Library, Bureau of Archives &
History

Major Theodore G. Ellis

Commander of the 14th Connecticut Volunteers. On 3 July, he led
the unit's second detachment, composed of sixty men, that attacked
the Bliss house to support Moore's command.

Credit: MOLLUS Collection at USAMHI

Adjutant Frederick B. Doten

A member of the 14th Connecticut Volunteers. He approached
Major Ellis with Sergeant DeForest's request to take some of Bliss'
chickens as the men torched the barn. In October 1863, Doten was
promoted to Captain of Company A.
Credit: MOLLUS Collection at USAMHI

Captain Samuel A. Moore

Co. F, 14th Connecticut Volunteers. Led the regiment's sixty
man detachment that charged the Bliss barn.

Credit: MOLLUS Collection at USAMHI

Captain James B. Coit

Co. K, 14th Connecticut Volunteers. During the afternoon of 2
July, he was run over by a runaway horse.
Credit: MOLLUS Collection at USAMHI

Captain John C. Broatch

Co. A, 14th Connecticut Volunteers. He and
Sergeant-Major Hincks witnessed the mortal
wounding of Private Thomas J. Brainard on 3 July.
Credit: Courtesy Tom Riemor

Sergeant-Major William B. Hincks

14th Connecticut Volunteers. He and Captain Broatch witnessed the mortal wounding of Private Brainard. Later, Hincks received a Congressional Medal of Honor for his conduct during Pickett's Charge.
Credit: MOLLUS Collection at USAMHI

1st Lieutenant Frederick J. Seymour

Co. C, 14th Connecticut Volunteers.
Credit: MOLLUS Collection at USAMHI

Major George Hopper

Commanded the 10th New York Battalion which served as the 3rd
Division's provost guard.
Credit: Washburn's *History of the 108th New York*

Colonel George Lamb Willard

Commanded 3rd Brigade, 3rd Division, 2nd Corps.
Though the exploits of his brigade during the afternoon
of 2 July (in which Willard was killed) are well known,
several of his units served on the Bliss Farm picket line
that morning and the following day.
Credit: MOLLUS Collection at USAMHI

Major Hugo Hildebrandt

Commanded the 39th New York Volunteers ("The Garibaldi Guards"), 3rd Brigade. Wounded near the Bliss Farm on 2 July, his regiment served there from 11 AM-12 Noon.
Credit: Roger D. Hunt Collection at USAMHI

Colonel Clinton MacDougall

Commanded the 111th New York Volunteers, 3rd Brigade. At least two companies served at the Bliss Farm between 11 AM and 4 PM, 2 July.
Credit: MOLLUS Collection at USAMHI

Captain James C. Lynch

Co. B, 106th Pennsylvania Volunteers. Commanded
the Philadelphia Brigade's advanced skirmish line on
2 July and led at least one of his company's attacks on
the Bliss barn approaching from the south.
Credit: USAMHI

2nd Lieutenant William H. Smith

Co. B, 106th Pennsylvania Volunteers. He was killed in
Captain Lynch's first attack on the Bliss barn.
Credit: USAMHI

Captain John G. Hazard

Commanded 2nd Corps Artillery Brigade.
Credit: MOLLUS Collection at USAMHI

Captain William A. Arnold

Commanded Battery A, 1st Rhode Island Light Artillery. Positioned immediately north of the "Bloody Angle," Arnold complained of sharpshooters' fire emanating from the Bliss barn. His complaints may have convinced Hays to order the burning of the farm buildings.

Credit: MOLLUS Collection at USAMHI

1st Lieutenant George Woodruff

Commanded Battery I, 1st U. S. Light Artillery. On 2 July, his guns, positioned in Zeigler's Grove, assisted in the repulse of Wright's Brigade and of the 48th and 19th Mississippi on the Union center. Woodruff was killed during Pickett's Charge.
Credit: USAMHI

160

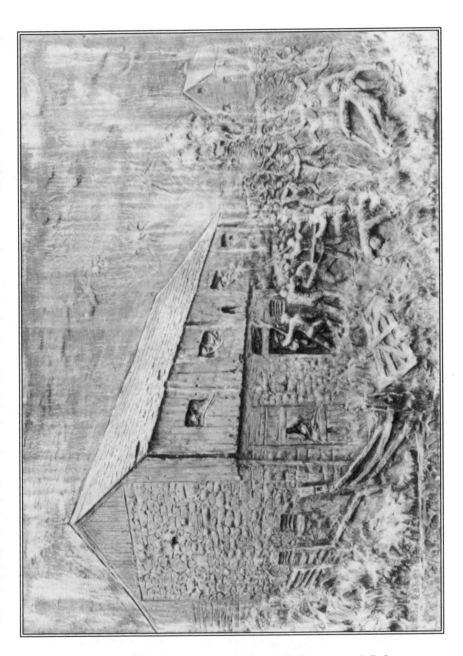

Attack of the 12th New Jersey on the Bliss barn 2 July.

12th New Jersey Volunteers Memorial, Hancock Avenue.
Credit: Author

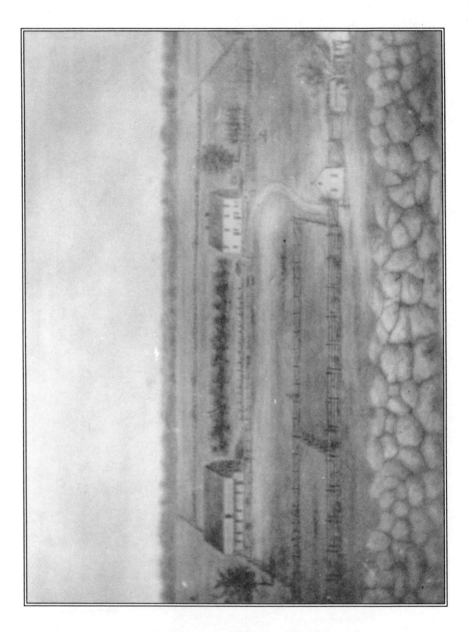

Artist's Rendition of the Bliss Farm in 1863.

Unknown artist, and undated. A water color painting once in the possession of the David Harris Family, descendants of Daniel B. Harris, William Bliss' son-in-law. Note the white Brian house in the foreground at lower right, and the Brian tenant house situated along the Emmitsburg Road immediately to the right of the Bliss Farm's access lane that is shaped like a question mark.

Credit: GETT/EISE Library

**Approximate Point of View of the Watercolor
Painting Cyclorama Observation Deck Looking West**

The Brian Orchard is in the foreground and the 12th New Jersey
Memorial's shaft seen on the west side of Hancock Avenue (cutting
across this view's foreground). The Bliss Farmstead is located
beyond the Emmitsburg Road (which is lined by utility poles). The
Bliss barn site is marked by the large clump of bushes directly
behind the pole, visible at photo-center. The line of trees beyond
marks the crest of Seminary Ridge.

Credit: Author

**View of the Brian Farm Buildings Taken for Matthew
Brady, o/a 15 July 1863**

Probably the earliest known photograph that shows some portion
of the Bliss Farm. The northern end of Bliss' orchard can be seen
in the middle distance at photo-right. Barely visible through the
trees, immediately to the right of the small frame structure, can be
seen the Brian tenant house.

Credit: MOLLUS Collection at USAMHI

View Looking North From the Bloody Angle Past the Brian Farm.

Arnold's Battery was located along the stone wall seen in the left foreground. The 1st Delaware, with the 14th Connecticut to its rear, was positioned along the continuation of the stone wall that runs from a point behind the saplings, seen in the foreground, to the Brian barn, seen above photo-center. The Brian house and orchard are to the right of the barn. Willard's Brigade was positioned behind a stonewall just off the right side of the photo. Oak Hill, the northern terminus of Seminary Ridge, is the dark feature located above and immediately to the left of the post-war house and barn. The post-war house, located on the eastern side of the broad, flat knoll's crest, still stands on the southwest corner of Johns and Culp Avenues in the Colt Park Development.

Credit: GETT/EISE Library

165

**View Looking Northwest From the Bloody Angle
Across the Northern Half of the Bliss Property
Towards the McMillan Farmstead.**

The bank of the Bliss barn is barely visible as two light specks seen just above the left-center border of the photo, and from that point to the right, the remnants of the Bliss orchard can be seen. The house site and the north end of the orchard are blocked from view by the large tree with the man leaning against its trunk. The Emmitsburg Road cuts across the center of this view where the tall trees can be seen in the middle ground above and right of the large trees in the foreground. McMillan Woods and their farm buildings are seen on the crest of Seminary Ridge as the dark strip to the left of the large tree in the foreground near its top and the white dots above the right-most tall tree along the Emmitsburg Road, respectively. The advanced skirmish line of the 8th Ohio was located at right-center, beyond the light-colored strip above the fence line seen in middle ground that is lined by a few short trees – approximately the crest of the broad, flat knoll.

Credit: GETT/EISE Library

View Looking Westerly From the Bloody Angle Across the Southern Half of the Bliss Farm.

The northwest corner of the Bloody Angle (the plowed field in the foreground) is seen left of center. Just above it, the Emmitsburg Road, seen cutting across this view, is lined by post and rail fences. The fence line seen running into the distance above the top of the third tree to the right of the Bloody Angle was recently rebuilt by the National Park Service and marked part of the southern boundary of the Bliss Farm. Today the Virginia State Memorial on Seminary Ridge stands just left of the point where that fence intersects the tree line in the distance.

Credit: GETT/EISE Library

167

**View of the Northern Half of the Bliss Farm Looking East From
McMillan Woods on Seminary Ridge Towards the Union Center
ca. 1910-1940.**

The Brian Farm buildings can be seen below and to the right of the old Zeigler's
Grove Observation Tower standing left of photo-center on the horizon – Cemetery
Ridge. The approximate northern boundary of the Bliss Farm is marked by the fence
line, which projects down and to the left from a point below the Brian buildings, to a
tree next to a white strip where it angles directly towards the camera position. The
white strip is the advanced skirmish line of the 8th Ohio. The Bliss Farm's western
boundary is approximately marked by the line that cuts across this view's center and
which ends just right of the tree in the left foreground – the southern terminus of the
Sunken Road located at the junction of the north and western boundaries. The bank
of the Bliss barn can barely be seen to the right of the top of the small tree and
immediately to the left of the large tree in the right foreground. The trees on
Cemetery Hill are seen on the horizon at photo-left.

Credit: GETT/EISE Library

168

View From the Brian House Looking West.

The Brian lane ran from the barn (photo-left), along the left side of the white post and rail fence, down to the Emmitsburg Road where the Brian tenant house once stood to the right of the white fence. Across the road, near the west end of the Brian lane, an access lane ran from the road "directly" to the Bliss Farm buildings. The Bliss barn site, marked by a large clump of bushes, can be seen at photo-center, above and to the left of the far end of the white fence.

Credit: Author

169

**View of the Bliss Farm Site Looking Southwest From
a Position 100 Yards South of the Left End of the
8th Ohio's Advanced Skirmish Line.**

The large clump of bushes marks the remains of the bank that led
to the first floor of the Bliss Barn. Barely visible to the left of the
bushes is the 14th Connecticut's "Center of Barn" marker, and at
the right end of the bank can be seen the 12th New Jersey's
advanced position marker. Barely visible near photo-right amid
some taller grass can be seen the 14th Connecticut's "Center of
House" marker. In the foreground, the small bushes mark the
location of Stevens Run, while the Virginia State Memorial is seen
on Seminary Ridge in the background.

Credit: Author

View Looking East Over the Bliss Farm From the North Carolina Memorial on Seminary Ridge.

The Gettysburg National Tower, at photo-left, marks the location of Cemetery Hill, while the famous "copse of trees" is located at far right on the crest of Cemetery Ridge. The bushes marking the Bliss barn site are seen in the middle ground just right of center. A portion of the broad, flat knoll is located below the tower where the trees and houses of Colt Park can be seen.

Credit: Author

171

**View Looking East From the Confederate Picket
Reserve Along the Western Boundary of the
Bliss Farm.**

Again, the bushes mark the bank of the Bliss barn on the east side
of the orchard. In the background, the Brian Farm buildings are
seen at photo-left, and the northwest corner of the Bloody Angle is
marked by the tree at photo-right. The utility poles mark the
location of the Emmitsburg Road.

Credit: Author

End Notes

1. William B. Wilson Diary (1800-1873), Bendersville (Pa.) From 1 January 1820 to 31 December 1871, copy on file, Adams County Historical Society, Gettysburg, PA (ACHS); and Gettysburg *Star and Sentinel*, dated 30 July 1885. See Henry Eyster Jacob's Letter to Editor, "Meteorology of the Battle: Notes by Rev. Dr. [Michael] Jacobs."

2. Sarah M. Broadhead, *The Diary of a Lady of Gettysburg, Pennsylvania From June 15-July 15, 1863*, unpublished manuscript, ACHS.

3. Margaretta Kendlehart McCartney, "A Story of Early's Raid", *Compiler*, Saturday, 30 June 1923; Wilber S. Nye, *Here Come the Rebels*, (Baton Rouge: Louisiana State University Press, 1965, Reprint Ed., Dayton, OH: Morningside House, Inc., 1984) p. 277.

4. Harriet Hamilton Baily, untitled, unpublished account, ACHS; and Lydia Catherine Zeigler Clare, "A Gettysburg Girl's Story of the Great Battle," not dated, ACHS.

5. Margaret McMillan, "History of the McMillan House on West Confederate Avenue, Gettysburg PA," dated 6 January 1941, unsigned transcript (?), McMillan Farm Historical Data, File 2-3a, Gettysburg National Military Park Library (GNMP/LIB), pp. 2 and 3.

6. George D. Bowen, "Diary of Captain George D. Bowen [12th New Jersey Regiment]", *Valley Forge Journal: A Record of Patriotism and Culture*, Valley Forge Historical Society, publishers; 11: #5, (June 1984), p. 130.

7. *Adams Sentinel* (Gettysburg), 11 August 1856, See farm sale advertisement: "Alexander Cobean offers for sale a farm of 44 acres 3/4 of a mile south of Gettysburg, with a double log and frame house,

weatherboarded, and a large brick bank barn, and other outbuildings; two wells of water near the house with pumps; with choice fruit [probably apples], and a variety of other fruit, consisting of peaches, cherries, and c. – 50 acres adjoining the above [also is for sale];" and Henry S. Stevens, *Souvenir of Excursions to the Battlefields By the Society of the 14th Connecticut Regiment and Reunion at Antietam, September, 1891*, (Washington, D. C.: Gibson Brothers, Printers and Bookbinders, 1893), pp. 16 and 17.

8. Stevens, *Souvenir 14th Connecticut*, p. 16.

9. Douglas Southall Freeman, *Lee's Lieutenants: A Study in Command*, 3 volumes, (New York: Charles Scribner's Sons, 1942), 2: pp. 278, 390 and 567; Patricia L. Faust, ed., *Historical Times Illustrated Encyclopedia of the Civil War*, (New York: Harper and Row, 1986), pp. 172 and 173; Ezra Warner, *Generals in Gray: Lives of the Confederate Commanders*, (Baton Rouge: Louisiana State University Press, 1956, 1986 ed.), p. 424; Walter Clark, ed., *History of the Several Regiments and Battalions from North Carolina in the Great War, 1861-65*, 5 volumes, (Raleigh: E. M. Uzzell, Printer and Bookbinder, 1901), 1: pp. 85 and 99; and The Confederate Magazine, (Wendall, NC: Broadfoots Bookmart, 1893), 2: p. 150.

10. Ibid.

11. *The War of the Rebellion: A Compilation of the Official Records of Union and Confederate Armies*, 128 volumes, (Washington, D. C.: U. S. War Department, 1880-1901), Vol. 27, pt. 2: pp. 669-71 (OR).

12. Division of Archives and History of North Carolina, *North Carolina Troops, 1861-1865: A Roster*, Weymouth T. Jordan, Jr., ed., Unit Histories by Louis H. Manain, (Raleigh: North Carolina Print Shop, 1985), 9: p. 285 and Clark, *History NC Troops*, 2: p. 692.

13. OR, Vol. 27, pt. 2: p. 671.

14. Clark, *History of NC Troops*, 2: p. 678.

15. Faust, *Encyclopedia*, p. 324; Ezra J. Warner, *Generals in Blue: Lives of the Union Generals*, (Baton Rouge: Louisiana State University Press, 1956), pp. 223 and 224.

16. Warner, *Generals in Blue*, p. 73.

17. Frederick H. Dyer, *A Compendium of the War of the Rebellion*, (New York: Thomas Yoseoff, special contents, Sagamore Press, 1959), 3 volumes, 3: pp. 1499 and 1500.

18. Faust, *Encyclopedia*, p. 700; and Warner, *Generals in Blue*, pp. 465 and 466.

19. Ibid.

20. William P. Seville, *History of the First Regiment Delaware Volunteers: From the Commencement of the "3-Month Service" to the Final Muster Out at the Close of the Rebellion*, Papers of the Historical Society of Delaware, (Wilmington: Historical Society of Delaware, 1884), pp. 32 and 33.

21. Ibid, p. 36; Dyer, *Compendium*, 3: p. 1017; Faust, *Encyclopedia*, p. 700; and Warner, *Generals in Blue*, pp. 465-67.

22. Ezra D. Simons, *A Regimental History: The One Hundred and Twenty-Fifth New York State Volunteers*, (New York: Judson Printing Co., 1888), pp. 188-219 and Dyer, *Compendium*, 3: pp. 1453 and 1454.

23. Ibid.

24. OR, 27 pt. 1: p. 453, Hays stated he was "assigned a position on a ridge, parallel with the [Taneytown] road facing westward....;" Thomas G. Murphy, *Four Years in the War: History of the First Regiment of Delaware Veteran Battles, Incidents, Promotions, the Names of All Officers and Men Which Have Been Connected with the Regiment from Its Organization in 1861 to the Close of the War, 1865*, (Philadelphia: James Glaxton, 1866), p. 116; and Seville, *1st DE*, p. 80. Both Delawarians indicated that Hancock's Corps was posted "left of Cemetery Hill."

25. *Letter from John L. Brady to John B. Bachelder*, dated 24 May 1886, John B. Bachelder Papers, New Hampshire Historical Society, on microfilm, GNMP/LIB. Bachelder was the Superintendent of Legends and Tablets for the Gettysburg Battlefield Memorial Association. This organization's land acquisitions eventually formed the nucleus of the present-day Gettysburg National Military Park; and John W. Busey and David G. Martin,

Regimental Strengths at Gettysburg, (Baltimore: Gateway Press, Inc. 1982), p. 43.

26. U. S. Department of Commerce, Bureau of the Census, 6th U. S. Census, 1860, Delaware; U. S. General Services Administration, National Archives and Records Service, Military Records Branch (NA), Civil War Union Pension Records, J. Louis Brady, 1st Delaware, 3-year.

27. *Brady to Bachelder*, p. 3. Brady seems to be the only Union officer that placed the 1st Delaware on the skirmish line in the early morning of 2 July, indicating that the regiment withdrew shortly before 10:00 AM and then advanced again. Though the official reports of Lieutenant Dent of the 1st Delaware and Colonel Smyth state that their respective commands arrived on Cemetery Ridge between 6:00 and 8:00 AM, Lieutenant Dent wrote that the 1st Delaware's first and only advance out to the skirmish line occurred at "8 AM," and they remained on picket until they were forced to withdraw in the afternoon around 4:00 PM which resulted in Colonel Harris' arrest.

In his letter to Bachelder, Brady recounted the activities of the 1st Delaware which he alleged were based on his "'Diary' for July 1863 in which all the leading events and movements... [of the regiment were] recorded on the Date of actual occurrence...." Unfortunately we do not know how detailed Brady was in his entries. Was each event recorded in proper sequence (as it happened)? Or did he write them in the evening recalling the day's activities? Moreover, we do not know how much Brady extemporized as he wrote to Bachelder twenty-three years later.

As the author read and re-read Brady's letter, the Delawarian's tone suggested that sour grapes were being squashed. Brady used six of the twenty-seven pages of the document to substantiate his claims that he was in command of his regiment from 2-17 July, though he never filed an official report.

At face value, Brady's preoccupation with the 1st Delaware's command structure casts doubt as to the integrity and the reliability of his account of the events of 2-3 July. However, upon the perusal of his application for a soldier's pension filed in the spring of 1889, one surmises that Brady was a stickler for details – he listed every one-horse town, from Philadelphia via Dog Run, Arkansas to Ashland, Virginia, where he and his family resided after his expiration of term of service on 8 August 1864. Moreover, Brady was fairly detailed as to the length of time spent at each location, listed the month and year of arrivals and departures. The level of Brady's detail in preparing his pension application suggests that his recollection of events may be fairly accurate though some occurrences still could be out of proper sequence.

Analysis of other documentation (noted later in this book) tends to contradict the sequence of events purported by Lt. Dent and Col. Smyth that a force, composed of some 250 men, remained intact until the late afternoon. Why would Hays, charged with protecting a sector of the main Union line only about 600 yards wide (from Cemetery Hill to the Copse of Trees), reinforce it with ten additional companies (about 300-400 men) about 11:00 AM when casualties were relatively light? Secondly, according to the official report of Confederate General Carnot Posey, Lieutenant C. W. Burrage of Company A, 19th Mississippi "was on picket with his company, and... had been beyond the orchard and barn, in the morning... [Emphasis added]." Posey's Mississippians did not arrive on Seminary Ridge opposite the Bliss Farm until sometime between 9:00-11:00 AM (roughly corresponding to Brady's timing of the 1st Delaware's withdrawal). Thus, if the 1st Delaware Regiment had been assigned to the skirmish line at 8:00 AM and did not withdraw until the afternoon, how could Lt. Burrage be beyond the barn in the morning?

Moreover, after the publication of the 1st Delaware's regimental history in 1884, Brady contacted the author, William P. Seville, about its accuracy. In his letter to Bachelder (10-12), Brady alleged that Seville wrote back to him stating that he had assumed Dent's official report was correct, but then thought that Brady's "diary is more likely to be right than the memories of those who decided in favor of Dent," which implies that Dent's official report (that had been submitted to Smyth so he could prepare his official report) was flawed.

28. Ibid.

29. NA, Pension Record, Edward P. Harris, 1st Delaware Regiment, 3-year.

30. NA, Pension Record, Charles B. Tanner, 1st Delaware, 3-year; and U. S. Army, *The Medal of Honor of the United States Army*, (Washington, D. C.: Government Printing Office, 1948), p. 117.

31. NA, Pension Record, Tanner.

32. *Brady to Bachelder*, pp. 4 and 5.

33. Ibid, p. 5.

34. NA, Pension Record, Ezeckiel P. Alexander, 1st Delaware, 3-year.

35. NA, Pension Record, John N. Ellegood, father of Martin W. B. Ellegood, 1st Delaware, 3-year, *Letter from Martin Ellegood to Julia (?)*, dated 2 March 1863.

36. Ibid.

37. Ibid. See *Letter from Martin Ellegood to Nat (?)*, dated 28 May 1863.

38. Ibid.

39. Historical Society of Delaware, Wilmington; Church Yard Records, St. Pauls Protestant Episcopal Church Cemetery, Georgetown, Delaware.

40. *Brady to Bachelder*, p. 5.

41. Edmund J. Raus, Jr., *A Generation on the March: The Union Army at Gettysburg*, (Lynchburg, Va.: H. E. Howard, Inc., 1987), p. 96.

42. OR, Vol. 27, pt. 1: p. 460.

43. William Kepler, Phd., *History of the "Three-Months" and "Three-Years" Service From April 16, 1861 to June 22, 1864 of the Fourth Regiment Ohio Volunteer Infantry in the War for the Union*, (Cleveland: Leader Printing Co., 1886), p. 126.

44. New York Monuments Commission for the Battlefields of Gettysburg and Chattanooga, *Final Reports on the Battlefield of Gettysburg*, (Albany: J. B. Lyon Co., 1900), 3 volumes, 2: p. 300.

45. Bachelder Papers. *Letter from Charles A. Richardson to John B. Bachelder*, dated 18 August 1889.

46. Chris Warner, *Union Infantry Uniforms*, (Surry, England: Almark Publishing Co., Ltd., 1977), p. 28.

47. Dyer, *Compendium*, 3: pp. 1418 and 1419.

48. Joseph Cantey Elliot, *Lieutenant General Richard Huron Anderson: Lee's Noble Soldier*, (Dayton, OH: Morningside Press, 1985), pp. 18 and 20; Faust, *Encyclopedia*, pp. 14 and 15; and Warner, *Generals in Gray*, pp. 8 and 9.

49. Elliot, *Anderson*, pp. 23 and 24.

50. Ibid, pp. 32-35, 39-56, and 58-60; Faust, *Encyclopedia*, pp. 14 and 15; Warner, *Generals in Gray*, pp. 8 and 9; and OR, Vol. 27, pt. 1: p. 275.

51. Faust, *Encyclopedia*, pp. 597 and 598.

52. Ibid; and OR, Vol. 12, pt. 2: p. 591.

53. Faust, *Encyclopedia*, pp. 597 and 598.

54. OR, Vol. 27, pt. 2: p. 633; James J. Kirkpatrick, *Diary of James J. Kirkpatrick*, The Center for American History, University of Texas at Austin, transcript on file, United States Army Military History Institute, (USAMHI) Robert L. Brake Collection; NA, Compiled Service Records, James J. Kirkpatrick, 16th Mississippi Infantry; and Austin C. Dobbins, *Grandfather's Journal: Co. B, 16th Mississippi Infantry, Harris' Brigade, Mahone's Division, Hill's Corps, Army of Northern Virginia, May 22, 1861 - July 15, 1865*, (Dayton: Morningside House, Inc., 1988), p. 148. Dobbins' ancestor wrote, "Around 10 A. M. we moved to an open field behind Pegram's Battery on Seminary Ridge, Wilcox to the right of Perry, Wright, Posey, with Mahone in reserve to the rear."

55. OR, Vol. 27, pt. 2: pp. 629 and 630. Report of Captain Charles Moffett corroborates the time of the brigade's arrival; Draughton S. Haynes, *The Field Diary of a Confederate While Serving With the Army of Northern Virginia*, (Darien, Ga.: The Ashantilly Press, 1963), p. 32; and NA, Compiled Service Records, Draughton S. Haynes, 49th Georgia Infantry.

56. *Richardson to Bachelder*, dated 18 June 1889.

57. Ibid.

58. William P. Haines, *History of the Men of Company F With Description of Their Marches and Battles of the 12th New Jersey Volunteers*, (Camden, NJ: C. S. Magrath, 1893), p. 38.

59. New Jersey Battlefield Commission 1886-1892, *Final Report of the Gettysburg Battlefield Commission of New Jersey*, (Trenton: John T. Murphy Publishing Co., 1891), p. 110.

60. *Bowen Diary*, pp. 128 and 129.

61. George Washburn, *A Complete History and Record of the 108th Regiment New York Volunteers: From 1862-1894 Together With Roster, Letters, Rebel Oaths of Allegiance, Rebel Passes, Reminiscences, Like Sketches, Photographs, etc., etc.*, (Rochester, NY: E. R. Andrews, 1894), pp. 48 and 49; and OR, 27 pt. 1: p. 478. See Captain Hazard's report.

62. *Final NY Report*, 1: p. 284.

63. OR, Vol. 27, pt. 2: p. 652. See Lieutenant Colonel Garnett's report.

64. Ibid, pp. 612 and 673. See Colonel R. Lindsey Walker's and Major Poague's reports, respectively.

65. Ibid, p. 663.

66. Dobbins, *Grandfather's Journal*, p. 148.

67. OR, Vol. 27, pt. 2: pp. 318 and 319.

68. Edwin B. Coddington, *The Gettysburg Campaign: A Study in Command*, (New York: Charles Scribner's Sons, 1968, Dayton, OH: Press of the Morningside Bookshop, 1979), pp. 187 and 188.

69. OR, Vol. 27, pt. 2: p. 633.

70. NA, Nathaniel H. Harris, 19th Mississippi Infantry; Faust, *Encyclopedia*, p. 424; and Warner, *Generals in Gray*, pp. 172 and 173.

71. OR, Vol. 27, pt. 2: p. 634.

72. Ibid, p. 633. In Dobbins, *Grandfather's Journal*, pp. 148 and 149, Dobbins' ancestor, describing the events of that afternoon, tends to corroborate Harris' statement that only half an hour passed before the 19th and 48th Mississippi advanced with General Wright's Brigade:

We held our position [on Seminary Ridge] until 3, when for an hour both sides began a terrific cannonading. At the height of the shelling a Confederate band stationed between Seminary and Cemetery Ridges (Wright's) began to play waltzes & polkas.... Around 6, 2 of our regiments (48th and 19th) moved forward as skirmishers. Later around 6:30, following Wright's Brigade, the 16th and 12th Miss. advanced across a road, through a hollow, and up the west slope of Cemetery Ridge. At times we advanced nearly to the batteries on the ridge, but the enemy, reinforced, forced us back. Around 6 we saw Gen. [William] Barksdale, riding a white horse, start up a hill near a peach orchard. As he charged, he took off his hat, put it on his sword, and waved it to his men to inspire them.

However, the accuracy of this account is in doubt. Did he actually have time to witness the attack of Posey's right wing advancing east of the Emmitsburg Road "nearly to the batteries on the ridge," when his regiment was involved in the fighting at the Bliss barn? Or was he referring to his regiment's advance towards the Emmitsburg Road and was "the enemy, reinforced" referring to the 8th Ohio on the broad, flat knoll? The sequence of terrain features (road, hollow, slope of Cemetery Ridge) could refer to: a Sunken Road that terminated at the northwest corner of the Bliss property, the Stevens Run stream bed, and the slope of the broad, flat knoll.

Secondly, Barksdale's Mississippi brigade of Longstreet's Corps attacked the famous Peach Orchard, located over a mile south of the Bliss Farm, and though his command wheeled northward, we believe that Barksdale moved no closer than a half mile of the Bliss Farm, thus how could any one in the 16th Mississippi, accurately identify Barksdale on horseback with his cap on his sword through the smoke of battle over a half mile away?

Lastly the Mississippian's use of the word "we" is uncertain. We suspect that his use may alternately refer to Posey's whole brigade, the 16th regiment, and Posey's right wing, or he could be referring to Confederates in general.

Unless Dobbins' relative was on detached service from the 16th, we speculate that he may have overheard conversations referring to the band, Barksdale's movements, and other stories after the fighting ended that day, and he included those episodes as he later wrote his diary entry for 2 July.

73. *Bowen Diary*, pp. 128 and 129.

74. Haines, *History Co. F, 12th NJ*, pp. 180 and 181.

75. Ibid; and NA, Combined Services Records, Henry F. Chew, 12th New Jersey Infantry, 3-year.

76. *Final NJ Report*, pp. 180 and 181.

77. Ibid, p. 227.

78. *Bowen Diary*, pp. 128 and 129.

79. *Final NJ Report*, pp. 110 and 111.

80. Ibid, p. 111.

81. NA, Nathaniel H. Harris, 19th Mississippi Infantry. See Letter from Captain H. S. Van Eaten to President Jefferson Davis, dated 1 February 1864, re: Samuel B. Baker.

82. *Bowen Diary*, pp. 128 and 129.

83. *Brady to Bachelder*, pp. 5 and 6. Although Brady had indicated to Bachelder that this meeting of Harris and Hancock occurred during the mid-morning hours, accounts of other soldiers do not verify his statement. Both Captain Chew (*Final NJ Report*, p. 111) and Sergeant Bowen (*Bowen Diary*, p. 129) of the 12th New Jersey specifically state that they had spoken to the lieutenant colonel of the 1st Delaware in the afternoon. Furthermore, the official report of the 1st Delaware filed by Lieutenant Dent (OR, Vol. 27, pt. 1: p. 469) inferred that the incident reported by Brady transpired in the afternoon.

It is impossible to ascertain how detailed Brady's diary entries are, when they were recorded, or how much he extemporized as he wrote to Bachelder twenty-three years after the battle. Also unknown is whether or not personality conflicts existed between the officers of the 1st Delaware which might explain the tone of Brady's letter. Moreover, would Harris be in command of a skirmish detail in the afternoon if he had been placed under arrest in the morning? Or would Hancock have arrested him in the afternoon after a good part of the 2nd Corps' skirmish line had fallen back under relatively light pressure when the situation on the Union left was deteriorating at an alarming rate? The latter scenario seems more likely.

84. Joseph R. C. Ward, *History of the One Hundred and Sixth Pennsylvania 2d Brigade, 2d Division, 2d Corps, 1861-1865*, (Philadelphia: F. MacManus, Jr. and Co., 1906), pp. 158 and 159.

85. Ibid.

86. Ibid, p. 190.

87. Ibid, p. 191.

88. NA, Pension Records, William H. Smith, 106th Pennsylvania Infantry.

89. OR, Vol. 27, pt. 1: p. 460.

90. NA, Pension Records, Peter Grubb, 4th Ohio Infantry, 3-year.

91. Kepler, *History 4th OH*, p. 127.

92. Raus, *Union Army*, p. 97.

93. NA, Pension Records, Franklin Sawyer, 8th Ohio Infantry, 3-year.

94. Franklin Sawyer, *A Military History of the Eighth Ohio Volunteer Infantry: The Battles, Marches, and Movements*, George A. Gout, ed., (Cleveland: Fairbanks and Co., 1881), p. 126.

95. Ibid, pp. 126 and 127. The Bachelder Maps of the Gettysburg Battlefield indicated that a worm fence was located on the western slope of the broad, flat knoll, running perpendicular to a post and rail fence that marked part of the northern boundary of the Bliss Farm.

96. Haines, *History Co. F, 12th NJ*, p. 38.

97. Dyer, *Compendium*, pp. 1361 and 1362.

98. Samuel T. Toombs, *New Jersey Troops in the Gettysburg Campaign: From June 5 to July 31, 1863*, (Orange, NJ: The Evening Mail Publishing House, 1888), p. 175; and NA, Pension Records, John T. Hill, 12th New Jersey Infantry.

99. OR, Vol. 27, pt. 1: p. 470; *Final NJ Report*, pp. 109 and 112; and *Letter From Corporal Christopher Mead, Company H, 12th New Jersey to His Wife*, dated 6 July 1863, Transcript, Brake Collection, USAMHI.

100. Washburn, *History 108th NY*, p. 49. Although Major Hill's official report and that of Lieutenant Colonel Sawyer indicated that the timing of their respective assaults were an hour apart, the personal accounts of Sawyer, Lieutenant Galway, and others of the 8th Ohio do not mention the charge of the 12th New Jersey. Surely the men of the 8th would have noted the ruckus that was created by the New Jerseyians' attack on the Bliss barn to their left and left front unless they were too preoccupied with their own charge on the Confederates at the Emmitsburg Road and the establishment of their advanced positions west of the Brian tenant house.

101. *Brady to Bachelder*, p. 6; and Ward, *History 106th PA*, p. 191.

102. William D. Henderson, *12th Virginia Infantry*, The Virginia Regimental Series, (Lynchburg, VA: H. E. Howard, Inc., 1984), pp. 106-167 and Benjamin H. Trask, *16th Virginia Infantry*, The Virginia Regimental Series, (Lynchburg, VA: H. E. Howard, Inc., 1986), pp. 73-128. Lists in these books indicate that at least twenty-three men from these units were killed, wounded, or captured on 2 July; and since Mahone's Brigade was not actively engaged that day, we suspect they were inflicted on the skirmish line at the Bliss Farm.

103. *Final NJ Report*, p. 112.

104. Washburn, *History 108th NY*, pp. 39, 48 and 49.

105. OR, Vol. 27, pt. 1: p. 470; and Inscription on the 12th New Jersey marker situated between the Bliss house and barn sites, Gettysburg Battlefield.

106. OR, Vol. 27, pt. 1: pp. 468 and 469; John K. Foster, *New Jersey and the Rebellion: A History of the Services of the Troops of New Jersey In and For the Union Cause*, (Newark: Martin R. Dennis and Co., 1868), p. 304; Frederick A. Jago, *12th New Jersey Volunteers: 1862-65*, (Haddenfield, NJ: Elmer Garfield Van Name, 1967), p. 8; *Mead to Wife*, dated 6 July 1863; and Toombs, *NJ Troops, Gettysburg*, p. 256. There were thirteen casualties in Company H.

107. *Final NJ Report*, pp. 112 and 113.

108. OR, Vol. 27, pt. 2: pp. 633 and 634.

109. Ibid, p. 634.

110. Ibid, p. 663.

111. *Brady to Bachelder*, p. 6. Brady mistakenly identifies the captain as Richard S. Thompson who actually led a second charge of the 12th New Jersey out to the Bliss barn the following morning; and *Letter from E. L. [Emerson L.] Bicknell to John B. Bachelder*, dated 6 August 1883, Bachelder Papers. Bicknell, a 2nd lieutenant in Andrew's Sharpshooters, suggests that the Confederates maintained a position within rifle range of Zeigler's Grove during the night of 2-3 July, in essence, firing from the area occupied by the 8th Ohio:

> The enemy... had the evening of the 2nd pushed up to the Emmitsburg Road and forced our lines back into a grove which ___ [ran?] along from the Taneytown Road west of the cemetery to the north point of Cemetery Ridge. I suppose it to be Zeiglers Grove. Having dug rifle pits during the night the enemy by firing from them drove our infantry out of the west end of the grove the next morning. [Bicknell] took 20 Sharpshooters and reoccupied the west front of the grove and held it all day.

Possibly, Bicknell's memory was foggy and he confused the Bliss Orchard with Zeigler's Grove. Though speculative at best, another interpretation of Bicknell's letter that would better conform with other Yankee accounts loosely suggests that Bicknell's company of sharpshooters was forced back from an advanced position west of the Emmitsburg Road, and later Confederate sharpshooters near the Bliss buildings dug rifle pits from which they peppered the Cemetery Ridge line, forcing Yankees away from the exposed western edge of Zeigler's Grove and the Brian Orchard. Indeed, several accounts, (documented later) indicated that Hays' troops were harassed by sharpshooters' fire emanating from the Bliss Farm buildings.

112. OR, Vol. 27, pt. 2: p. 634. See Posey's and Harris' reports.

113. Busey and Martin, *Regimental Strengths*, p. 189.

114.   *Kirkpatrick Diary*, p. 55; NA, Compiled Service Records, Kirkpatrick; and Dobbins, *Grandfather's Journal*, p. 148.

115. Busey and Martin, *Regimental Strengths*, p. 189.

116.   Coddington, *Gettysburg*, pp. 421 and 759, see note #63 referencing the addendum of Cadmus Wilcox to Lee as quoted in Douglas Southall Freeman, *R. E. Lee: A Biography*, 4 volumes, (New York: Charles Scribners, 1935), III: p. 555.

117. OR, Vol. 27, pt. 2: p. 621.

118. OR, Vol. 27, pt. 2: p. 658.

119. Ibid, p. 659. Dr. Henry E. Shepherd in his "Gallant Sons of North Carolina" that appeared in Confederate Veteran Magazine (Vol. 27: p. 413) quoted a statement allegedly made by Lee two months after the battle: "Had Pender remained in the saddle half an hour longer, we should have carried the field."

120.   8th Ohio Regimental Association, *The 8th Ohio at Gettysburg: Address of General Franklin Sawyer at the Reunion at Columbus, Ohio 1888*, (Washington, D. C.: E. J. Gray, 1889), pp. 4 and 5.

121. Ibid.

122. Ibid.

123. Kepler, *History 4th OH*, pp. 127 and 128.

124. Ibid, p. 128.

125. Haskin, Brevet Major William Lawrence, Captain 1st Artillery, *History of the First Regiment of Artillery: From Its Organization in 1821 to January 1, 1876*, (Portland, Me.: Thurston and Co., 1879), p. 169.

126. Theodore Reichardt, *Diary of Battery A, 1st Rhode Island Artillery*, (Providence, RI: N. Bangs Williams, 1865), p. 95.

127. Busey and Martin, *Regimental Strengths*, p. 84.

128. OR, Vol. 27, pt. 2: p. 634.

129. Ibid, pp. 622-24.

130. Ibid, p. 635.

131. Dobbins, *Grandfather's Journal*, p. 149.

132. See casualty statistics for Willard's brigade, OR, Vol. 27, pt. 1: p. 177.

133. Kepler, *History 4th OH*, p. 127.

134. NA, Pension Records, Peter Grubb; and Kepler, *History 4th OH*, pp. 127 and 131.

135. NA, Compiled Service Records, Addison H. Edgar, 4th Ohio Infantry, 3-year.

136. Kepler, *History 4th OH*, p. 270.

137. *Letter from William D. Seville to John B. Bachelder*, no date, Bachelder Papers; and OR, Vol. 27, pt. 1: p. 741.

138. Washburn, *History 108th NY*, p. 55.

139. Charles D. Page, *History of the Fourteenth Regiment, Connecticut Volunteer Infantry*, (Meriden, CT: The Horton Printing Co., 1906), p. 17.

140. Page, *History 14th CT*, pp. 21-25.

141. Ibid, pp. 62-69, 107, and 119-22; and Busey and Martin, *Regimental Strengths*, p. 43.

142. NA, Pension Records, Henry S. Stevens, 14th Connecticut Infantry.

143. Page, *History 14th CT*, p. 124.

144. Stevens, *Souvenir 14th CT*, p. 11.

145. Richard S. Thompson, "A Scrap of Gettysburg" in Ken Bandy and Florence Freeland, ed., *The Gettysburg Papers*, (New Materiels, Dayton, OH:

Press of the Morningside Bookshop, 1978), 2: p. 956. Thompson mistaken-ly identified the Union sharpshooters as Berdan's men.

146. Stevens, *Souvenir 14th CT*, pp. 11 and 12.

147. Bachelder Papers, *Letter from Theodore G. Ellis to John B. Bachelder*, dated 21 January 1884; and Stevens, *Souvenir 14th CT*, p. 15.

148. 8th Ohio, *8th Ohio at Gettysburg*, p. 5.

149. Thomas Francis Galway, *The Valiant Hours: Narrative of "Captain-Brevet" An Irish-American in the Army of the Potomac*, Wilbur S. Nye, ed., (Harrisburg, Pa.: Stackpole Books, 1961), p. 107.

150. Susan W. Benson, ed., *Berry Benson's Civil War Book: Memoirs of a Confederate Scout and Sharpshooter*, (Athens, Ga: University of Georgia Press, n. d.), p. ix.

151. Ibid, pp. 47 and 48.

152. Stevens, *Souvenir 14th CT*, p. 15.

153. Dobbins, *Grandfather's Journal*, p. 149; and Capt. E. Howard McCaleb, "Featherston-Posey-Harris Mississippi Brigade," *New Orleans Picaynue*, 1 June 1902 printed in Southern Historical Society Papers, Vol. 32: p. 335.

154. OR, Vol. 27, pt. 1: pp. 154 & 467.

155. OR, Vol. 27, pt. 2: pp. 155 & 320.

156. Coddington, *Gettysburg*, pp. 456 and 457; and OR, Vol. 27 pt. 2: pp. 156 & 359.

157. Stevens, *Souvenir 14th CT*, p. 15.

158. OR, Vol. 27, pt. 1: pp. 468 and 469.

159. *Brady to Bachelder*, p. 14.

160. Ibid.

161. Ibid.

162. Frederick Fuger, *Battle of Gettysburg: A Personal Re-Collection of That Battle*, Alexander Stewart Webb Papers, Yale University Library, Transcript on file USAMHI, Robert L. Brake Collection, p. 20. Fuger's account indicated that this exchange took place the morning of the second day of battle. Since the battery was not present at Gettysburg on 1 July, we suspect that he probably meant 3 July, their second day under enemy fire. The previous day, when Cushing's battery arrived near the Copse of Trees about 8:00 AM, the 1st Delaware had possession of the farmstead. Throughout the afternoon, Union skirmish lines were present on the Bliss Farm. After 4 PM, the attacks of the 8th Ohio, 12th New Jersey, and 106th Pennsylvania, and the subsequent occupation of the buildings until the Confederate attacks by Wright and Posey at 6:00-7:00 PM, all prevented Cushing from firing.

Apparently, Cushing's artillerists opened fire on the barn about the time Brady and his little band of Delawarians and Jerseymen had been forced back by the Southerners in the barn on 3 July, and as Cushing's fire chased the Johnnies out of the barn, this drew counter-battery fire from the Confederates that resulted in detonation of Cushing's three limbers.

163. Article in the Burlington (Vermont) *Free Press and Times*, 2 June 1911. Transcript in Brake Collection, USAMHI.

164. OR, Vol. 27, pt. 1: p. 478; and Haskin, *History 1st US Art.*, p. 169.

165. Stevens, *Souvenir 14th CT*, p. 17.

166. NA, Pension Records, William A. Arnold, Battery A, 1st Rhode Island Light Artillery.

167. Stevens, *Souvenir 14th CT*, p. 17.

168. OR, Vol. 27, pt. 1: p. 470; and *Final NJ Report*, pp. 110 & 115.

169. NA, Pension Records, Richard S. Thompson, 12th NJ Infantry.

170. *Brady to Bachelder*, pp. 14 and 15.

171. Haines, *History Co. F, 12th NJ*, p. 39; *Final NJ Report*, pp. 109 and 110.

172. Haines, *History Co. F, 12th NJ*, pp. 39 and 40.

173. Thompson, *Gettysburg Papers*, 2: pp. 957 and 958.

174. Haines, *History Co. F, 12th NJ*, pp. 39 and 40.

175. *Final NJ Report*, pp. 111 and 112.

176. Haines, *History Co. F, 12th NJ*, pp. 153 and 154.

177. *Final NJ Report*, pp. 111 and 112; and Haines, *History Co. F, 12th NJ*, p. 40.

178. Major Hill indicated a major and an enlisted man were captured (OR, Vol. 27, pt. 1: p. 470); Account of Charles D. Lippincott, Co. F, dated 22 January 1887, indicated "we captured but three" (*Final NJ Report*, p. 117); and *Letter of Richard S. Thompson*, dated 1863. A short time after the battle, Thompson wrote a letter in which he indicated that four Confederates had been captured. The original letter (as of 1989) was in the possession of Ralph and Gerry Poriss, 100 W. Kingswood Drive, Williamsburg, VA 23185.

179. Haines, *History Co. F, 12th NJ*, pp. 207 and 208.

180. Thompson, *Gettysburg Papers*, 2: p. 958.

181. *Final NJ Report*, p. 113.

182. Thompson, *Gettysburg Papers*, 2: p. 958.

183. *Final NJ Report*, p. 113.

184. Sawyer, *History 8th OH*, p. 129.

185. Thompson, *Gettysburg Papers*, 2: p. 958.

186. Sawyer, *History 8th OH*, p. 129.

187. Haines, *History Co. F, 12th NJ*, pp. 40 and 113.

188. Haines, *History Co. F, 12th NJ*, pp. 141-46; and 5th U. S. Census, 1850, Gloucester County, New Jersey.

189. Haines, *History Co. F, 12th NJ*, pp. 146 and 147; and 5th U. S. Census.

190. Haines, *History Co. F, 12th NJ*, pp. 147 and 148; and 5th U. S. Census.

191. Haines, *History Co. F, 12th NJ*, p. 148; and 5th U. S. Census.

192. Haines, *History Co. F, 12th NJ*, p. 98.

193. Ibid, p. 40; and Sawyer, *History 8th OH*, p. 129.

194. *Brady to Bachelder*, p. 15.

195. OR, Vol. 27, pt. 2: p. 673.

196. Ibid.

197. Ibid.

198. Ibid, pp. 673 and 674.

199. Ibid, p. 652.

200. *Kirkpatrick Diary*, p. 55.

201. Stevens, *Souvenir 14th CT*, p. 16.

202. Ibid.

203. Charles D. Page, *History of the Fourteenth Regiment Connecticut Volunteer Infantry*, (Meriden, CT: Horton Printing Co., 1906), p. 142 and 143.

204. OR, Vol. 27, pt. 1: p. 403; *Report of the Joint Committee to Mark the Position Occupied by the 1st and 2nd Delaware Regiments at the Battlefield of Gettysburg*, (Dover: The Delawarean Office, 1887), p. 19; and 2nd Delaware Volunteer's "Skirmish Line, July 3, 1863" Marker, North Hancock Avenue, GETT/EISE. A discrepancy exists when these two accounts and the current placement of the 2nd Delaware's skirmish line marker are compared. The regiment, part of the 4th (Brooke) Brigade, 1st (Caldwell)

Division, 2nd Corps, was heavily engaged on 2 July in the fight for the Wheatfield and Rose Woods. Numbering about 230 (Busey and Martin, p. 38), the unit lost about 100 men during the entire battle. According to the official report of Colonel William P. Baily, dated 15 August 1863, at 4 AM on 3 July the unit was moved "to the left and front, and formed line of battle behind the crest of a hill." Baily also mentioned that the enemy artillery bombarded his position "with great vigor," and that he advanced his command:

> 60 yards to the front where [they] threw up breastworks. At 9 a.m. Captain Evans, of Company A, was detailed with 30 men to picket our front. During the day he sent in 64 prisoners chiefly from North Carolina and Georgia regiments. The enemy kept up a constant and rapid fire of shot and shell on our position from 5 a.m. until 4 p.m. ....

In the Delaware Joint Committee's report on the placement of their markers and memorials at Gettysburg, the address of William H. Brady (a lieutenant and adjutant of the regiment) appeared in which he stated that:

> During the night the command was moved to the right and occupied a position left of center where Pickett's famous charge took place the next day.... The regiment was deployed as skirmishers for the brigade front....

Brady's account coincides with the Joint Committee's comment that they were going to place a "tablet" near the Jacob Hummelbaugh Farm.

However, the current placement of the regiment's skirmish line marker (the same location indicated on the Gettysburg National Park Commission's Map, "The Battlefield of Gettysburg," dated 1912) is situated about 100 yards south of the Brian Barn, between the 1st Delaware's and 12th New Jersey's memorials – right of center where Pickett's Charge took place. Secondly, though some of Wright's Georgians probably were active along the Confederate skirmish south of the Union center, where did the North Carolinians come from? Or were the Georgians and North Carolinians captured by the 2nd Delaware on the skirmish line part of the brigades of Thomas, Lane, and/or Scales?

One possible scenario roughly correlates the discrepancies. After the fight on 2 July, the 2nd Delaware was initially positioned near the Hummelbaugh Farm with the remainder of Brooke's Brigade. Since the regiment numbered only about 100 men, it may have been combined or ordered to cooperate with the 1st Delaware. If this was the case, Captain

Evans and Company A may have served on the skirmish line near the Bliss Farm.

205. *Letter From Samuel C. Armstrong to John B. Bachelder*, dated 6 February 1884, John B. Bachelder Papers.

206. Washburn, *History 108th NY*, p. 52.

207. Stevens, *Souvenir 14th CT*, pp. 17 and 18.

208. Ibid, p. 18; and OR, Vol. 27, pt 1: pp. 467 and 468.

209. NA, Compiled Service Records, Theodore G. Ellis, 14th Connecticut Infantry.

210. Page, *History 14th CT*, p. 119.

211. Ibid, p. 107.

212. Stevens, *Souvenir 14th CT*, p. 18.

213. Busey and Martin, *Regimental Strengths*, p. 203.

214. Stevens, *Souvenir 14th CT*, p. 18.

215. Page, *History 14th CT*, p. 16.

216. OR, Vol. 27, pt. 1: p. 651.

217. According to Henry S. Stevens, the order to break and run was given by General Hays, see H. S. Stevens and J. W. Knowlton, *Address Delivered at the Dedication of the Monument of the Fourteenth Connecticut Volunteers at Gettysburg, July 3rd, 1884 by H. S. Stevens and J. W. Knowlton*, (Middletown, CT: -----, 1884), p. 18. Eight years later Stevens repeats the story that the men were "to 'go as you please' or scatter and run," but does not indicate from whom the order was received, see Stevens, *Souvenir 14th CT*, p. 18.

218. Stevens, *Souvenir 14th CT*, p. 18.

219. Stevens and Knowlton, *Address 14th CT*, p. 19.

220. Stevens, *Souvenir 14th CT*, p. 19.

221. Stevens and Knowlton, *Address 14th CT*, p. 19. A shortened version appears in *Souvenir 14th CT*, p. 19.

222. NA, Compiled Service Records, Thomas J. Brainard, 14th Connecticut Infantry, 3-year.

223. Several hours later, another soldier took unnecessary risks. Brigadier General Richard S. Garnett, commanding a brigade in Pickett's Division, found himself in a similar situation. A year earlier, at the Battle at Kernstown during the Valley Campaign, Garnett's reputation as a competent officer had been questioned by Stonewall Jackson. Though Jackson was gone, allegedly Garnett felt honor-bound to recoup what he perceived had been lost through Jackson's allegations, and though he felt poorly after being kicked by a horse, Garnett led his brigade on horseback in Pickett's Charge. Possibly, actions taken by both Garnett and Brainard were attempts to disprove allegations of unsoldier-like conduct that they had felt were unjustly made against them.

224. Stevens, *Souvenir 14th CT*, p. 19.

225. Henry P. Goddard, *14th Connecticut Volunteers Reminiscences of the War of the Rebellion*, (Middletown, CT: C. W. Church, 1877), p. 13.

226. Stevens, *Souvenir 14th CT*, p. 19.

227. Ibid, pp. 19-21.

228. Edward P. Alexander, Southern Historical Society Papers, Vol. 4: p. 103.

229. *Ellis to Bachelder*, dated 3 November 1870.

230. Stevens, *Souvenir 14th CT*, p. 20.

231. Ibid.

232. Goddard, *14th CT*, p. 13.

233. Benson, *Berry Benson*, p. 48.

234. Thomas M. Littlejohn, "Recollections of a Confederate Soldier," Manassas National Battlefield Collection, Transcript on file GNMP/LIB.

235. Bachelder Papers, *Letter From "2nd Lt." Charles A. Hitchcock to John B. Bachelder*, 2 February 1886. Though the assignment of two couriers to carry the message to the 14th Connecticut seems logical – the chances for the order to reach its destination are doubled – we are skeptical about Hitchcock's account. Speculating that it was reasonable to assume that combustible materials (like hay and straw) could be found in the barn, why did Hitchcock scrounge for paper? Moreover, why did he look for matches to light the fire? He could have used black powder and percussion caps.

236. NA, Compiled Service Records, J. Parke Postles, 1st Delaware Infantry, 3-year.

237. W. F. Beyer and O. F. Keydel, eds., *Deeds of Valor; From the Records on File in the Archives of the United States Government: How American Heroes Won the Medal of Honor*, 2 volumes, (Detroit: Perrien-Keydel Co., 1907), 1: pp. 228 and 229.

238. Ibid.

239. Bachelder Papers, *Letters From O. B. Sawyer to John B. Bachelder*, dated 20 September 1870.

240. *Hitchcock to Bachelder*, p. 3.

241. Beyer et al, *Deeds of Valor*, 1: pp. 229 and 230. Postles also related a conversation he later allegedly had with a Confederate prisoner near the Brian House:

> "Well sir, I guess your time hain't come yet." Upon my asking why, he said, "Well, I had three fair shots at you, and there are plenty more fellows here who had as many." I had been so close to them when I passed the house... that they had recognized me....

However, the accuracy of Postles' account of his famous ride is suspect. Though ca. 1907 he stated the day was 2 July and that some "forty prisoners" were captured, in actuality twice that number were cornered in the Bliss barn (not the house) by the 12th New Jersey that afternoon. Nonetheless, Seville's history of the 1st Delaware (*1st DE*, p. 84) and Stevens' account

(*Souvenir, 14th CT*, p. 20) indicated Postles' ride took place the following morning <u>after</u> only as many as four Confederates were captured by Thompson's detachment of the 12th New Jersey. Stevens also indicated (p. 18) that the house "which had not figured much in former attacks, now [became] quite formidable...," further suggesting Postles' ride took place on 3 July. If not pure fabrication, Postles' account of the details of his ride, written forty-four years after the fact, actually may be a montage of his Gettysburg memories.

242. National Archives, Compiled Service Records, Postles.

243. Bachelder Papers, *Affidavit From James A. Stroazzi to John B. Bachelder*, dated 5 October 1870.

244. Stevens, *Souvenir 14th CT*, p. 22; *Ellis to Bachelder*.

245. Stevens, *Souvenir 14th CT*, p. 21; *Hitchcock to Bachelder*.

246. Stevens, *Souvenir 14th CT*, p. 22. "It is still a conundrum with us [in 1893] what became of Al. DeForest's chicken."

247. OR, Vol. 27, pt. 2: p. 651.

248. Stewart, *Pickett's Charge*, p. 185. See the illustration, "The Advance." In 1991 the National Park Service reconstructed that very fence line.

249. OR, Vol. 27, pt. 2: pp. 650 and 651.

250. OR, Vol. 27, pt. 1: p. 469. See Lieutenant Dent's report.

251. Stevens, *Souvenir 14th CT*, pp. 21 and 22.

252. James I. Robertson, *General A. P. Hill: The Story of a Confederate Warrior*, (New York: Random House, 1987), p. 219.

253. Elliot, *Anderson*, p. 16.

254. Ibid, p. 20.

255. Freeman, *Lee's Lieutenants*, 1: p. xix.

256. Ibid, 1: p. 192.

257. Ibid, 3: p. xxxviii.

258. Elliot, *Anderson*, p. 152.

259. OR, Vol. 27, pt. 2: p. 608.

260. Ibid, p. 614.

261. NA, Compiled Service Records, Samuel D. Shannon. Captain Shannon is a will-o'-the-wisp figure in the story of the Bliss Farm. Appointed captain of Company B, Lucas' South Carolina Battalion of Artillery on 6 June 1861, within five months he resigned his commission. However, by the late summer of 1862, R. H. Anderson had nominated him for appointment as his aide-de-camp, but that September, Anderson revoked the nomination. What is puzzling, in early December 1862 Anderson again requested Shannon's appointment and a month later he became an aide-de-camp. Serving with Anderson nearly a year, and mentioned in his report on Gettysburg with the rest of his staff who "rendered valuable services at all times and upon all occasions," on 15 December 1863 Shannon requested a twenty-day extension of a leave he had been granted on the 8th, and the following February his leave was extended an additional twenty days. Apparently, Shannon ran afoul with his commander, for on 21 October 1864 Anderson applied for the arrest and detention of his aide-de-camp. However, by November 1864 Shannon is addressed in the records as an acting assistant adjutant-general and is mentioned as such as late as Lee's surrender at Appomattox.

262. Freeman, *R. E. Lee*, III: p. 555.

Bibliography

General Sources

Arnold, James N. *Vital Records of Rehoboth, 1642-1896: Marriages, Intentions, Births, Deaths, with Supplements Containing the Records of 1896, Colonial Returns, Lists of Early Settlers, Purchases, Freemen Inhabitants, the Soldiers Serving in Phillip's War and the Revolution.* Providence, RI: Narragansett Historical Publications Co., 1897.

Bandy, Ken and Freeland, Florence. *The Gettysburg Papers.* New Materials Dayton, OH: Press of the Morningside Bookshop, 1978.

Beyer, W. F. and Keydel, O. F., eds. *Deeds of Valor: From the Records in the Archives of the United States Government: How Americans Won the Medal of Honor.* 2 Vol., Detroit: Perrien-Keydel Col., 1907.

Bliss, Leonard, Jr. *History of Rehoboth, Bristol County Massachusetts Comprising a History of the Present Towns of Rehoboth, Seekonk, and Pawtucket From Their Settlement to the Present Time; Together With Sketches of Attleborough, Cumberland, and Part of Swansey and Barrington to the Time That They Separated From the Original Town.* Boston: Otis, Broaders, and Co., 1836.

Bowen, Richard LeBaron. *Early Rehoboth: Documented Historical Studies of Families and Events in Plymouth Township.* 4 Vol., Concord, MA: Rumford Press, 1945.

Busey, John W. and Martin, David G. *Regimental Strengths at Gettysburg.* Baltimore: Gateway Press, 1982.

Coddington, Edwin B. *The Gettysburg Campaign: A Study in Command.*

New York: Charles Scribner's Sons, 1968; Reprint Ed. Dayton, OH: Morningside Bookshop, 1979.

Coggins, Jack. *Arms and Equipment of the Civil War*. Illustrated by author. Garden City, NY: Doubleday and Co., 1962.

Downs, John B. and Healey, Fenwick Y., ed. *History of Chautauqua County, New York and Its People*. 2 Vol., Boston: American Historical Society, Inc., 1921.

Duffy, James N.; Krueger, Goltfried; and Corbin, William H. *Final Report of the Gettysburg Battlefield Commission of New Jersey*. New Jersey Gettysburg Battlefield Commission Reports. Trenton: John T. Murphy Publishing Co., 1891.

Dyer, Frederick H. *A Compendium of the War of the Rebellion*, 3 Vol., New York: Thomas Yoseoff. Special Contents; Sagamore Press, 1959.

Elliot, Joseph Cantey. *Lieutenant General Richard Heron Anderson: Lee's Noble Soldier*. Dayton, OH: Morningside Press, 1985.

Faust, Patricia L., ed. *Historical Times Illustrated Encyclopedia of the Civil War*. New York: Harper and Row, 1986.

Freeman, Douglas Southall. *Lee's Lieutenants: A Study in Command*. 3 Vol., New York: Charles Scribner's Sons, 1942.

Georg, Kathleen R., ed. *The Location of the Monuments, Markers and Tablets on the Gettysburg Battlefield*. Gettysburg: National Park Service, Gettysburg National Military Park, 1982.

Hassler, Warren W., Jr. *Crisis at the Crossroads: The First Day at Gettysburg*. University, AL: University of Alabama Press, 1970.

Krick, Robert K., ed. *The Gettysburg Death Roster: The Confederate Dead at Gettysburg*. 2nd Edition, Revised. Dayton, OH: Morningside Bookshop, 1985.

Higginson, Thomas Wentworth. *Massachusetts Soldiers and Sailors of the Revolutionary War*. Boston: Wright and Potter Printing Co., 1896.

Mahan, D. H. *An Elementary Treatise on the Advanced-Guard, Outposts, and the Detached Service of Troops and Manner of Posting and Handling Them in the Presence of the Enemy.* New Edition, New York: John Wiley, 1861; Reprinted Corinth, MS: C. D. Jarnagan, 1985.

Morris, Richard B. *The American Revolution Reconsidered.* New York: Harper and Row, 1967; First Harper Torchbook Ed., 1968.

New York Monuments Commission for the Battlefields of Gettysburg and Chattanooga. *Final Reports on the Battlefield at Gettysburg.* 3 Vol., Albany: J. B. Lyon Co., 1900.

Nye, Wilber S. *Here Come the Rebels.* Baton Rouge: Louisiana State University Press, 1965; Dayton, OH: Morningside House, Inc., 1984.

Pennsylvania Gettysburg Commission. *Pennsylvania at Gettysburg: Ceremonies at the Dedication of the Monuments.* Harrisburg: William Stanley Ray, State Printer, 1904.

Raus, Edmund J., Jr. *A Generation on the March: The Union Army at Gettysburg.* Lynchburg, VA: H. E. Howard, Inc., 1987.

Robertson, James I., Jr. *General A. P. Hill: The Story of a Confederate Warrior.* New York: Random House, 1987.

Stewart, George R. *Pickett's Charge: A Microhistory of the Final Attack at Gettysburg, July 3rd, 1863.* Boston: Houghton Mifflin Co., 1957; Reprint Ed., Dayton, OH: Morningside House, Inc., 1983.

Tilton, Rev. George H. *A History of Rehoboth, Massachusetts; Its History For 215 Years, 1643-1918 in Which is Incorporated the Vital Parts of the Original History of the Town Published 1836, and Written by Leonard Bliss, Jr.* Boston: Louis E. Crosscup Co., 1918.

Toombs, Samuel T. *New Jersey Troops in the Gettysburg Campaign: From June 5 to July 31, 1863.* Orange, NJ: The Evening Mail Publishing House, 1888.

Tucker, Glenn. *High Tide at Gettysburg: The Campaign in Pennsylvania.* New York: Bobbs Merrill Co., Inc., 1958.

United States Army. *The Medal of Honor of the United States Army.*

Washington, DC: Government Printing Office, 1948.

United States War Department. *The War of the Rebellion: A Compilation of the Official Records of the Union and Confederate Armies.* 128 Vol., Washington, DC: U. S. Government Printing Office, 1880-1901.

Warner, Ezra J. *Generals in Blue: Lives of Union Commanders.* Baton Rouge: Louisiana State University Press, 1959; 1977 Printing.

Warner, Ezra J. *Generals in Gray: Lives of Confederate Commanders.* Baton Rouge: Louisiana State University Press, 1959; 1978 Printing.

Young, Andrew W. *History of Chautauqua County, New York: From Its First Settlement to the Present Time.* Buffalo: Matthews and Warren, 1875.

Unit Histories

Banes, Charles H. *History of the Philadelphia Brigade.* Philadelphia: J. B. Lippencott and Co., 1876.

Caldwell, James F. J. *The History of a Brigade of South Carolinians Known First as Gregg's and Subsequently as McGowen's Brigade.* Philadelphia: King and Baird, Printers, 1866; Reprint Ed., Dayton, OH: Morningside Bookshop, 1974.

Delaware, Joint Committee. *Report of the Joint Committee to Mark the Positions Occupied by the 1st and 2d Delaware Regiments at the Battlefield of Gettysburg, July 2d and 3d, 1863.* Dover: -----, 1887.

Dunlop, William S. *Lee's Sharpshooters or the Forefront of Battle.* Little Rock, AR: Tunnan and Pittard, Printers, 1899.

Eighth Ohio Regimental Association, ed. *The Eighth Ohio at Gettysburg: Address by General Franklin Sawyer, Reunion at Columbus, Ohio 1888. Roster of Survivors.* Washington, DC: H. J. Gray, 1889.

Goddard, Henry P. *14th Connecticut Volunteers Regimental Reminiscences of the War of the Rebellion.* Middletown, CT: C. W. Church, Steam Printers, 1877.

Haines, William P. *History of the Men of Company F With Description of the Marches and Battles of the 12th New Jersey Volunteers.* Camden, NJ: C. S. Magrath, 1897.

Hall, Isaac. *History of the Ninety-Seventh Regiment, New York Volunteers (Conklin Rifles) in the War for the Union.* Utica, NY: L. C. Childs and Son, 1890.

Haskin, William L. *History of the First Regiment of Artillery: From Its Organization in 1821 to January 1, 1876.* Portland, ME: Thurston and Co., 1879.

Henderson, William D. *12th Virginia Regiment.* First Ed., Virginia Regimental Series. Lynchburg, VA: H. E. Howard, Inc., 1984.

Hussey, George A. *History of the Ninth Regiment N. Y. S. M. – N. G. N. Y. S. (83rd New York Volunteers); 1845-1888.* William Todd, ed., New York: J. S. Ogilvie, 1889.

Jago, Frederick. *12th New Jersey Volunteers, 1862-65.* Haddenfield, NJ: Elmer Garfield Van Name, 1967.

Kepler, William. *History of the "Three Months" and "Three Years" Service From April 16th, 1861 to June 22nd, 1864 of the Fourth Ohio Volunteer Infantry in the War for the Union.* Cleveland: Leader Printing Co., 1886.

Murphy, Thomas G. *Four Years in the War: The History of the First Delaware Veteran Volunteers (Infantry) Containing an Account of the Marches, Battles, Incidents, Promotions, the Names and Men Who Have Been Connected With the Regiment From Its Organization in 1861, to the Close of the War, in 1865.* Philadelphia: James S. Glaxton, 1866.

Page, Charles D. *History of the 14th Regiment, Connecticut Volunteer Infantry.* Meriden, CT: The Horton Printing Co., 1906.

Sawyer, Franklin. *A Military History of the 8th Regiment Ohio Volunteer*

Infantry: Its Battles, Marches, and Army Movements. George A. Root, ed., Cleveland: Fairbanks and Co., 1881.

Seville, William P. *History of the First Delaware Volunteers: From the Commencement of the "Three Months Service" to the Final Muster-Out at the Close of the Rebellion.* Vol. 4, Papers of the Historical Society of Delaware. Wilmington: Historical Society of Delaware, 1884.

Simons, Ezra D. *A Regimental History: The One Hundred and Twenty-Fifth New York State Volunteers.* New York: Judson Printing Co., 1888.

Stevens, Henry S. *Souvenir of Excursions to the Battlefields by the Society of the Fourteenth Connecticut Regiment and Reunion at Antietam September 1891: With History and Reminiscences of Battles and Campaigns of the Regiment on the Fields Revisited.* Washington, DC: Gibson Brothers, 1893.

Stevens, H. S. and Knowlton, J. W. *Address Delivered at the Dedication of the Monument of the 14th Connecticut Volunteers at Gettysburg, Pa. July 3rd, 1884.* Middletown, CT: -----, 1884.

Trask, Benjamin H. *16th Virginia Regiment.* First Ed., Virginia Regimental Series. Lynchburg, VA: H. E. Howard, Inc., 1986.

Wallace, Lee A., Jr. *A Guide to Virginia Military Organizations 1861-65.* 2nd Revised Ed., Lynchburg, VA: H. E. Howard, Inc., 1976.

Ward, Joseph R. C. *History of the One Hundred and Sixth Pennsylvania 2d Brigade, 2d Division, 2d Corps, 1861-1865.* Philadelphia: F. MacManus, Jr. and Co., 1906.

Washburn, George H. *A Complete Military History and Record of the 108th Regiment, New York Volunteers: From 1862 to 1894 Together with Roster, Letters, Rebel Oaths of Allegiance, Rebel Passes, Reminiscences, Life Sketches, Photographs, etc., etc.* Rochester, NY: E. R. Andrews, 1894.

Willison, Arabella M. *Disaster, Struggle, Triumph: The Adventures of 1,000 "Boys in Blue," From August 1862 to June 1865.* Albany: The Argus Co., 1870.

Unit Rosters

Bates, Samuel P. *History of Pennsylvania Volunteers, 1861-5.* 5 Vol., Harrisburg: B. Singerly, State Printer, 1869.

Clark, Walter, ed. *History of the Several Regiments and Battalions From North Carolina in the Great War.* 5 Vol., Raleigh, NC: E. M. Uzzell, 1901.

Connecticut: Adjutant-General's Office. *Catalogue of Connecticut Volunteer Organizations With Additional Enlistments and Casualties Compiled From Records in the Adjutant-General's Office.* Hartford: Case, Lockwood & Co., 1864.

Connecticut: Adjutant-General's Office. *Catalogue of Connecticut Volunteer Organizations (Infantry, Cavalry, Artillery) in the Service of the United States, 1861-1865, With Additional Enlistments, Casualties etc. etc. and Brief Summaries Showing Operations and Service of the Several Regiments and Batteries.* Hartford: Brown and Gross, 1869.

Connecticut: Adjutant-General's Office. *Record of Service of Connecticut Men in the Army and Navy of the United States During the War of the Rebellion.* Hartford: The Case, Lockwood, and Brainard Co., 1889.

Foster, John Y. *New Jersey and the Rebellion: A History of the Services of the Troops and Its People in and for the Union Cause.* Newark: Martin R. Dennis Co., 1868.

Higginson, Thomas Wentworth. *Massachusetts in the Army and Navy, 1861-65.* Boston: Wright and Potter Printing Co., 1896.

McKinley, William, Jr.; Taylor, Samuel M.; and Howe, James C., ed. *Official Roster of the Soldiers of the State of Ohio in the War of the Rebellion, 1861-1866.* 12 Vol., Akron: The Werner Co., 1893.

Moore, John W., ed. *Roster of North Carolina Troops in the War Between the States.* 4 Vol., Raleigh: Ashe and Gatling, 1882.

Phisterer, Frederick. *New York in the War of the Rebellion, 1861 to 1865.* 5 Vol. and Index, 3rd Ed., Albany: J. B. Lyon Co., 1912.

New York: Adjutant-General's Office. *A Record of the Commissioned, Non-Commissioned Officers and Privates of the Regiments Which Were Organized in the State of New York and Called Into Service of the United States to Assist in Suppressing the Rebellion Caused by the Succession of Some of the Southern States From the Union, A. D. 1861, As Taken From the Muster-In Rolls on File in the Adjutant-General's Office, S. N. Y.* 8 Vol., Albany: Comstock and Cassidy, 1864.

New York: Adjutant-General's Office. *Annual Report of the Adjutant-General of the State of New York for the Year 1893.* 40 Vol., Albany: J. B. Lyon Co., 1894.

Rietti, J. M. C., ed. *Military Annals of Mississippi: Military Organizations Which Entered Service of the Confederate States of America From the State of Mississippi.* Jackson, MS: -----, n. d.; Reprint Spartansburg, SC: The Reprint Co., 1976.

Salley, A. S., ed. *South Carolina Troops in Confederate Service.* 3 Vol., Columbia: The R. L. Bryan Co., 1913.

Stryker, William. *Record of Officers and Men on New Jersey in the Civil War.* 2 Vol., Trenton: John L. Murphy Steam Book and Job Printers, 1876.

Tompkins, D. *14th South Carolina Volunteers.* Charlotte, NC: Observer Printing and Publishing House, 1897.

Published Diaries and Personal Narratives

Alleman, Mrs. Tillie Pierce. *At Gettysburg or What a Girl Saw and Heard of the Battle: A True Narrative.* New York: W. Lake Borland, 1889; Reprint, Baltimore: Butternut and Blue, 1987.

Benson, Susan W., ed. *Berry Benson's Civil War Book: Memoirs of a Confederate Scout and Sharpshooter.* Athens, GA: University of Georgia Press, n. d..

Bowen, George D. "Diary of Captain George D. Bowen." *Valley Forge*

Journal: A Record of Patriotism and Culture. Vol. 11, #1. Valley Forge Historical Publishers, June 1984.

Brown, Varina D. *A Colonel at Gettysburg and Spotsylvania.* 2 Parts. Columbia, SC: The State Co., 1931.

Fiske, Samuel W. *Mr. Dunn Brown's Experiences in the Army.* New York: C. S. Felt, 1866.

Galway, Thomas F. *The Valiant Hours: Narrative of "Captain-Brevet," An Irish-American in the Army of the Potomac.* Wilber S. Nye, ed. Harrisburg, PA: Stackpole Books, 1961.

Harris, Captain W. M., compiler. *Movements of the Confederate Army in Virginia: And the Part Taken Therein by the Nineteenth Mississippi Regiment From the Diary of Gen. Nat H. Harris.* Duncansby, MS: Capt. W. M. Harris, 1901.

Haynes, Draughton S. *The Field Diary of a Confederate Soldier While Serving with the Army of Northern Virginia.* Darien, GA: The Ashantilly Press, 1963.

McCartney, Margaretta Kendlehart. "A Story of Early's Raid." Gettysburg (Pa.) *Republican Compiler*, Saturday 20 June 1923.

Reichardt, Theodore. *Diary of Battery A, 1st Rhode Island Light Artillery.* Providence, RI: N. Bang Williams, 1865.

Southern Historical Society Papers. 49 Vol., Southern Historical Society.

Unpublished Diaries, Letters, Manuscripts, and Papers

Baily, Harriet Hamilton. *Account of the Battle of Gettysburg.* n. d.

Bachelder, John B., Papers. New Hampshire Historical Society.

Broadhead, Mrs. Sarah M. "The Diary of Gettysburg, Pa. From June 15 - July 15, 1863."

Clare, Lydia Catherine Zeigler. "A Gettysburg Girl's Story of the Great

Battle."

Fenton Historical Society Archives, Jamestown, NY.

Fuger, Frederick. "Battle of Gettysburg and Personal Recollections of That Battle." Alexander Stewart Webb Papers. Yale University Library.

Kirkpatrick, James J. "Diary of James J. Kirkpatrick." The Center for American History, University of Texas at Austin.

Littlejohn, Thomas M. "Recollections of a Confederate Soldier." Manassas National Battlefield Collection.

McCurdy, Charles M. "Gettysburg: A Memoir."

McMillan, Margaret. "History of the McMillan House (Originally 'Wildwood')," dated 6 January 1946.

Mead, Christopher. *Letter From Corporal Christopher Mead, Company H, 12th New Jersey to His Wife*, dated 6 July 1863.

O'Neal, John W. C. *Record of Confederate Burials: Journal of Dr. John W. C. O'Neal, M. D.*

Raus, Edmund J., Jr. *Union Civil War Burials at Gettysburg.*

Scott, Winfield, Captain, Company C, 126th New York. "Pickett's Charge: As Seen From the Front Line." California Commandary, Military Order of the Loyal Legion of the United States.

Thompson, Richard S. Letters.

Wilson, William B. Diary.

Government Documents and Records

Adams County, Pennsylvania. Office of the Register and Recorder, Gettysburg, Pa.

Adams County, Pennsylvania. Tax Records, 1807-1953.

Bradford County, Pennsylvania. Office of the Register and Recorder, Towanda, Pa.

Bristol County, Massachusetts. Registry of Deeds, Taunton, Mass.

Bristol County, Massachusetts. Registry of Probate, Taunton, Mass.

Chautauqua County, New York. Deed Records, Mayville, NY.

Chautauqua County, New York. County Mapping Department, Mayville, NY.

Pennsylvania, Commonwealth of. Department of the Auditor-General, Damage Claims Under the Acts of April 23, 1863, April 9, 1869, and May 27, 1871.

U. S. Department of Commerce, Bureau of the Census. Population Census 1830, 1840, 1850, and 1860.

U. S. Department of Commerce, Bureau of the Census. General Services Administration, National Archives and Records Service, Military Records Branch.

Newspapers

Burlington (Vt.) *Free Press and Times.*

Gettysburg (Pa.) *Adams Sentinel.*

Gettysburg (Pa.) *Republican Compiler.*

Gettysburg (Pa.) *Star and Banner.*

Maps

Bachelder, John B., Situation & Topographic Maps of the Gettysburg Battlefield.

Gettysburg National Park Commission, "The Battlefield of Gettysburg,"
    1912.

U. S. Geological Survey, 7.5 Minute Series, Gettysburg and Fairfield
    Quadrangles.

Warren, Gouverneur K., Commission. Maps of the Gettysburg Battlefield.

Miscellaneous

Bliss, James. *Headstone of Dr. James Bliss*. Village Cemetery, Bay Stone
    Road, Rehoboth, Bristol County, Massachusetts.

Bliss, William. *Bliss Family Memorial*. Evergreen Cemetery, Sinclairsville,
    Town of Charlotte, Chautauqua County, New York.

Civil War Times Illustrated Magazine.

The Confederate Veteran Magazine.

U. S. Army Military History Institute, Archives.

INDEX